# GLIMPSES OF THE FAMOUS

# GLIMPSES OF THE FAMOUS

*Seventy brief and personal conversations*

CHRIS HEAL

Published by Chattaway and Spottiswood
Four Marks, Hampshire
www.candspublishing.org.uk

chrisheal@candspublishing.org.uk

All rights reserved. No part of this publication may be reproduced, stored in a retrieval system or transmitted, in any form or by any means, electronic, mechanical, photocopying, recording or otherwise, without prior permission in writing from the publisher.

© Chris Heal, 2025

The moral right of Chris Heal to be identified as the author of this work has been asserted.

The names, characters and quotes of the principal characters, events and incidents are memories of the author, except where stated otherwise.
Opinions about events, characters and organisations are the views of the author.

A catalogue record for this book is available from
the British Library.

ISBN 978-1-9161944-9-6

Design and typeset: Mary Woolley, www.battlefield-design.co.uk
Cover design: Paul Hewitt, www.battlefield-design.co.uk
Print liaison and website: Andy Severn, www.oxford-ebooks.com
Printed on demand: www.ingramspark.com

To Adrian,
best hospital mate,
for his sanity-saving humour
and
for the creative spark for this book
and the road to recovery

# CONTENTS

| | Page |
|---|---|
| Introduction | 13 |
| **John Fellows Akers**<br>Chief Executive Officer, IBM | 17 |
| **George Alan Ashman**<br>Manager, West Bromwich Albion Football Club, *and*<br>**Richard Asa Hartford**<br>Scottish football international | 21 |
| **Michael Antony Aston**<br>English archaeologist and *Time Team* star, *and*<br>**Charles Nicholl**<br>English author of history, biography and literary detection | 25 |
| **Odd Ingolf Bakke**<br>Norwegian WWII resistance fighter | 29 |
| **Shirley Veronica Bassey**<br>Welsh singer | 33 |
| **Allan Robert Border**<br>Australian cricket batsman and captain | 37 |
| **Roelof Frederik 'Pik' Botha**<br>South African Minister of Foreign Affairs, *and*<br>**Jeremy Bernard Corbyn**<br>Leader of the Labour Party and the UK's Opposition, *and*<br>**John Enoch Powell**<br>British politician, scholar and writer | 41 |

**James Gordon Brown** 47
Scottish UK Prime Minister

**James Burke** 51
English broadcaster, science historian, author, *and*
**Sir Ludovik Henry Coverley Kennedy**
Scottish journalist and author

**Mangosuthu Gatsha Buthelezi** 55
Zulu prince, KwaZulu Chief Minister

**William Henry Chattaway** 59
English sculptor who lived in Paris, *and*
**Deborah Garman**
Daughter of the Bloomsbury Set & the UK Communist Party

**Daniel Marc Cohn-Bendit** 65
French-German student revolutionary leader

**John Julius Cooper, 2nd Viscount Norwich** 69
English historian, travel book writer and TV performer, *and*
**'Forgotten'**
Celebrated British actress

**Thomas Frederick Cooper** 73
Welsh comedian

**Édith Jeanne Thérèse Cresson** 75
French Prime Minister

**Pete Crew** 79
English rock climber

**Nguyen Sinh Cung** 83
Ho Chi Minh, 'Uncle Ho', President, Democratic Republic of Vietnam

**Reginald Kenneth Dwight** 87
Sir Elton Hercules John, British singer and songwriter

**Sir Stephen John Fry** 89
English actor, comedian and presenter

**Erich Ernst Heinrich Gerth** *and*     91
**Georg Carl Gerth**
WWI Kapitänleutnants, u-boat commanders and brothers

**Qaddura Mohammed Abd Al-Hamid**     95
Moroccan terrorist and hotel bomber

**Chester 'Chet' Bayard Hansen**     99
Aide to US General of the Army Omar Bradley, WWII

**Sir Jack Arnold Hayward**     103
English businessman, philanthropist, owner of
Wolverhampton Wanderers, *and*
**Graeme Murray Walker**
English motorsport commentator, *and*
**Sir Bernard Ingham**
Margaret Thatcher's chief Press secretary

**Paul David 'Bono' Hewson**     107
Irish singer songwriter and activist, *U2* rock band, *and*
**Sir George Ivan 'Van the Man' Morrison**
Irish musician

**Jeffrey Owen Hawkes**     113
South African golfer, *and*
**Anthony Alastair Johnstone**
Zimbabwean golfer and Sky Sports commentator

**Ronald Edmund Hutton**     117
English professor of history at Bristol University

**Alun Arthur Gwynne Jones**     123
Baron Chalfont, Welsh journalist and politician

**Nigel Kennedy**     127
English violinist

**Patrick 'Maxie' Lane**     129
English sculptor, artist and author

**Sir Edwin Ronald Nixon**     133
Chief Executive, IBM UK; Chairman, Amersham International, *and*

**Sir Leonard Harry Peach**
Head of Personnel & Corporate Affairs, IBM UK;
Chief Executive, NHS Management Board

**Anthony Nolan**   139
Young sufferer from rare inherited blood disorder

**Chukwuemeka Odumegwu Ojukwu**   145
President of Biafra, *and*
**Frederick McCarthy Forsyth**
English novelist and journalist

**Ian Richard Kyle Paisley**   155
Baron Bannside, Protestant religious leader, Northern Ireland

**Alan Peter Pascoe**   159
British Olympic Games hurdler and businessman, *and*
**Dame Darcey Andrea Bussell**
English ballerina, *and*
**Sir Martin Stuart Sorrell**
British businessman; founder of WPP advertising firm

**Colin Trevor Pillinger**   163
English planetary scientist; *Beagle 2* Mars lander

**Michael John Procter**, *and*   167
**Clive Edward Butler Rice**
South African cricket allrounders

**Major The Reverend W David Raths**   171
Canadian canon of the Cathedral of the Most Holy Trinity, Bermuda

**Jon Silkin**   173
British poet; founder of *Stand* magazine

**Guy Slater**   177
English writer, theatre and TV director, *and*
**Peter Duncan**
*Blue Peter* presenter and Charlie Chaplin in *Little Tramp*, the musical, *and*

**Lord Richard Samuel 'Dickie' Attenborough**
English actor, film director and producer, *and*
**Brian Blessed**
English actor, *and*
**Sir Cameron Anthony Mackintosh**
British theatrical producer and theatre owner

**Laurence Soper** (et al) 183
Monks, priests and abusers at St Benedict's School, Ealing

**Alec James Stewart** 187
English international batsman, wicket-keeper and captain, *and*
**David Ivon Gower**
English international batsman and captain

**John Thomson Stonehouse** 191
British parliamentarian who faked his own death

**Lhamo Thondup** 195
Jetsun Jamphel Ngawang Lobsang Yeshe Tenzin Gyatso,
14th Dalai Lama

**Paul Tortelier** 199
French cellist and composer

**Siaosi Tāufaʻāhau Tupoulahi** 201
Tāufaʻāhau Tupou IV, King of Tonga

**Harry Waxman** 205
English cinematographer

**Prince Charles Philip Arthur George Windsor** 209
King Charles III, *and*
**Nigel Corbally-Stourton**
Irish hunting and fishing soldier and royal go-between

# INTRODUCTION

Many people have at least one bad year. Mine, 2024, lasted for some eighteen months: a laser stone operation that went wrong, failed corrective surgery which put paid to a kidney, hallucinatory urinary infections, sepsis, falls without the energy to rise, jammed face against the wall in an A&E corridor without care for twelve hours, diabetes wildly out of control, weeks in hospital and, finally, a major heart attack.

Even worse, my brain emptied and I could barely walk while clutching a Zimmer frame. I realised that my days as an author had ended. So had the idea that I would ever read a book again or that I could claw back the necessary imagination and stamina to fill an empty screen with creative writing.

Adrian in the bed opposite began to mock our sterile hospital surroundings, sufficiently disrespectful, unaccepting and ribald enough to shock parts of the ward and a few straight-laced staff. However, it was enough to delight the majority and to keep me sane.

As our beds guarded the ward entrance, we became a gauntlet for any intruder, pompous or pleasant, friend or foe. We began to tell stories of personal victories and failures from our pasts. Little went unchallenged. Adrian often accused me of exaggeration and name-dropping.

As I lay, desperate for sleep, mind fuddled, often depressed, I played games of counting. How many countries had I visited? How many types of animals eaten? How many famous people had I met?

What did I mean by 'famous'? I decided they would all be in *Wikipedia* even though, by itself, it might be a questionable qualification.

What did I mean by 'met'? I felt that could mean fleeting conversations, but with clearly personal moments of engagement.

I got to over fifty luminaries. Later, at home, it was soon over seventy, nudging one for every year that I had lived.

Was this an average number for an ordinary person born seventy-seven years ago without family privilege and titled cousins? I still don't know, but it is a game anyone can play quietly alone or with family at home.

What did strike me was the breadth of 'famousness', not all my recalled meetings were with, for instance, cricketers, industrialists or politicians.

After a few weeks out of hospital, shorn of confidence and direction, an idea was born. I would write a simple book with a just a few pages detailing each of my seventy encounters, an arbitrary limit. For each, I would add a little extra research, background, a picture and context. Very personal, off-beat, whacky even. It would be no great novel. Just for me, really.

It would be a 'dipping' book where one could follow one's fancy of famous person and find only a few pages to read. While the stories would be autobiographical, the book would not be a story of my life. Many other important or interesting events had taken place with family or 'ordinary' people, or while I was alone.

In fact, some of my 'famous' encounters were trivial and signified nothing other than I had met someone with a past others deemed important. The book's sole purpose would be to dredge my memory and to drag me back into the land of my living imagination. I realised that there was another, more important book, unresearched and unwritten, *Glimpses of Ordinary People*, who had individually changed my life by some act or advice.

However, as the weeks went by, the acts of research and writing dug even more from my memory and, even as the page proofs came in, I had a list of well over one hundred. There were close decisions on who to leave out: John Browne, chief executive of BP, at his London headquarters; Jacques Cousteau, French inventor of the underwater breathing apparatus, in Glasgow; Oliver Gilkes, historian and archaeologist, at Butrint in Albania; Tasmin Little, English classical violinist, in East Germany; Professor Bill Manning, archaeologist, at Troy, western Turkey; Godwin Vella, Heritage Malta, at the Ġgantija Temples, Gozo; Iolo Williams, Welsh ornithologist and author, at Brecon Beacons, as well as a host of international rugby players met, particularly at Heriot's at Goldenacre, Edinburgh, and at Leicester Tigers at Welford Road.

As a result of checking my definition of famousness, I have quoted liberally, when appropriate and without attribution, from *Wikipedia* (anathema, I admit, for some), especially for details of supporting events which were unknown to me, and possibly partial and flawed, and for which I say 'thank you' and have made a suitable financial contribution.

The events covered by the chapters in this book go back over sixty years, if it is imaginable, to a time when there was no internet. I have remembered and researched as best I can and sometimes left things vague where there is serious doubt. There must inevitably be errors in date, place or sequence. When criticisms are made, it is because that is my recall and I believe it is important to the story. Only one personal slight is intended. If any other upset is caused, I apologise.

Chris Heal
Four Marks, Hampshire
2025

# JOHN FELLOWS AKERS

## Chief executive officer, IBM

Powerful men have a way of displaying their authority. I've met a few and how they do it has always interested me. For some, it seems to ooze from their pores. It's natural, immediate, and depending on the situation can be quickly frightening. For others, you can soon see the sham. Their bravado, bullying perhaps, comes from their position, what they think they can do to you, and not from any innate ability. Few are good leaders over time, just short-term hustlers. The trick is binary: to stand your ground or to leave altogether.

*John Akers.* IBM Newsroom.

John Akers had power and he had position. He also had a fearsome reputation as a sharp mind that scattered fools and the timid to the winds. This was his first year as chief executive officer of the IBM Corporation after winning a serious board room battle. Now he led over 400,000 souls spread across the world. It was mooted, none too quietly, that he thought that was far too many people. Jobs were not as secure as they used to be.

My problem was that Mr Akers, sir, was upset and I was the only IBM employee within firing range.

It was 1985. We were standing in the grounds of the PACE (Planned Advancement of Community Education) Commercial College in Soweto, the apartheid township near Johannesburg in South Africa. PACE was a showcase secondary school, conceived and funded by several large American businesses, led by IBM. Opened in 1981, it was an elite facility intended to prepare black youngsters for universities or the business world. Seven million dollars had provided well qualified instructors and the latest in computer equipment.

Local activists and the South African government both recognised that the Americans were making a real and visible commitment to bettering the lives of young black people. About six hundred pupils had enrolled at PACE with only a ten per cent drop out. The first class was about to graduate.

That's why Akers was there: to lead the graduation, to announce further funding and to arm himself with ammunition for the vociferous disinvestment community back in the USA.

That hot early morning, as I sat on the edge of my bed in my shorts, I received a phone call saying that my director was sick and would not be able to guide Akers through the event. I was due to be there anyway, but my work was later, after the ceremony, when I would marshal a small group of local journalists.

'Would I please get over to Soweto at once in order to host Akers?'

Akers was a man I had never met although, of course, I knew the stories. The college was not a place I had ever visited. I knew little of the arrangements. I should be honest. My director was a man who did seem to fall ill when the pressure was on and discretion might save the day. I suspected a trap that needed a fall guy.

I got there as quickly as a family car can go. Akers saw me arrive, recognised the suit, and came over to me. He had been talking to the college principal and a couple of senior government officials.

'I've been here over an hour,' he spat, just loud enough for no one else to hear. 'For most of that time, I've been on my own sitting in the car. How come I got given the wrong time?'

I felt the power. I also realised why I was needed as a patsy.

What do you do? I apologised, then checked that he knew the agenda, when he had to speak and for how long, and was happy with the introductions he had been forced to make himself. I reminded him that I needed twenty minutes at the end of the ceremony for short press interviews.

'Where's your director?' he asked.

'Sudden sickness,' I said.

Akers gave me a long stare. 'Well, at least you didn't lead on that.' I felt a glimmer of possible survival.

I escorted him back to the dignitaries. They were all relaxed in true South African style and Akers was soon laughing and joking.

The local journalists were tongue tied or indifferent. I make a short introduction and asked for any questions. The chap from *The Sowetan*, a liberation struggle newspaper, asked something inane and that was that. I think they were all more interested in getting to the sandwiches. There was enough material anyway in the press release.

My next problem remained. The South African computer trade newspaper, widely read, was represented by a journalist who was well known to me and, to be frank, pleasant but often a pain in the proverbial. The opportunity to get at Akers exclusively was a huge attraction to him. Reluctantly, I had agreed to a solo interview, but only if the journalist stayed on topic and didn't get too technical. He had promised agreement faithfully on pain of excommunication and I knew he was lying.

Steve Jobs, the founder of Apple, had said in a recent interview that Akers was a 'smart, eloquent, fantastic salesperson, but he didn't know anything about product'. The all-powerful, ultra-safe and often vindictive press office in IBM's headquarter in the US had bent my ear for an hour on the self-same subject the day before. I was to be in full protect mode. The future of the universe and my place in it, depended on the outcome.

With young people slouching everywhere, a quiet spot was hard to find. I had to lead both men through corridors to a far classroom. By the time we arrived, and perched on school desks, I could see Akers thought this treatment was not suitable to his rank. I wasn't sure if it was the glower he gave me or the piercing eyes that worried me most.

From my perspective, the interview was a disaster. The journalist broke every rule in the book and completely ignored our preparatory discussions. I decided to kill him. I thought once to interrupt and to close the meeting down, but Akers seemed to relax into the conversation. At twenty minutes, I did cut in, but Akers allowed a further ten before I forcibly reminded him of his schedule. I led him back to his car, but he didn't say 'Goodbye'.

Two days later, the newspaper appeared with the Akers interview as front page lead. And also in the next week. And the next. Copies of the stories were faxed to the wolves at HQ.

For the next few weeks, I waited for an avalanche of criticism from within the company in South Africa and in the USA.

None came. The silence was loud and filled my office. My director evaded me for a month and when we finally met the whole visit was ignored.

Shortly afterwards, IBM disinvested from South Africa, alongside General Motors and Coca-Cola. 'The corporate exodus from South Africa seemed to have begun in earnest.'[1]

Frequently, disinvestment did not interrupt profit flows. Companies like IBM did not close up shop but sold, leased or half-gifted their operations to local businessmen or to their employees, maintaining a presence through licensing agreements, distribution contracts and technology transfers. There were often back door loopholes which allowed a return if conditions improved.

The truth was that American companies employed only a small portion of South Africa's black workforce, about fifty thousand people, about one per cent. The major impact of their departure was on domestic politics rather than in the townships.

By this time, Soweto's schools were in chaos and PACE was no exception.[2] In fact, its special status made it a particular target for young militants. White teachers had their car tyres slashed and the campus was raided by security forces. Many student were forced to flee. The stars and stripes was publicly burned after a meeting with American businessmen. Late in 1986, PACE suspended teaching.

Akers was credited with simplifying IBM's bureaucracy. In 1988, he announced a sweeping restructuring to reverse three years of disappointing performance. The company was to decentralise, thousands of employees had to switch jobs He also cut the workforce by fifty thousand. At the same time, Akers was on the board of Lehman Brothers when it filed for bankruptcy.

In 1993, Akers was forced to resign in a coup that reached back to his own assumption of office. There was widespread dismay at the falling share price among traditional supporters like the major banks.

John Akers died of a stroke, aged seventy-nine, in Boston in 2014.

---

1  Massing, Michael, 'South Africa: The Business of Fighting Apartheid', *The Atlantic,* 2/1987.
2  Ditto.

# GEORGE ALAN ASHMAN

Manager, West Bromwich Albion Football Club

# RICHARD ASA HARTFORD

Scottish football international

*Alan Ashman, 1968, FA Cup win.*
Birmingham Post and Mail.

*Asa Hartford.*

Alan Ashman was a big man in West Bromwich as manager of the local first division football club. He knew my father, the town's head postmaster, through the Rotary Club. I wasn't so big. I was a very new reporter on the local weekly newspaper, the *Midland Chronicle*.

'You're a bloody idiot,' Ashman said directly to my face and in front of a dozen others. We were standing in West Bromwich Albion's training ground clubhouse. 'You can't even spell. Call yourself a reporter.'

Ashman used to play for Carlisle United, but was forced to retire through injury. He ran the poultry farm of one of the club's directors while, on the side, he managed Penrith, an amateur team. In 1963, Third Division Carlisle needed a new manager quickly. Too late to prevent that season's relegation, Ashman won promotion for the next two years and then finished third in his new league. He was scooped up by Albion in 1967. We had our conversation soon after he joined the club. The following year, his team would win the FA Cup.

I was at the training ground to report on an early afternoon game by Albion's junior team which played in a local youth league. At full time, I had to phone in a two hundred and fifty word story which effectively meant just listing the goals and the teams. Because I didn't really follow football, I was always rushing to get the players' names right. This perk was for the *Birmingham Post and Mail* which published a sports edition each Saturday afternoon. It meant a steady cheque for three guineas a home game.

My crime? A unknown Scottish player named Hartford had just joined Albion's staff from Drumchapel Amateurs. I heard his first name and, because he had scored two goals in the game, I had called him 'Acer' in my press copy instead of 'Asa'. Honestly, I had never heard of the Scottish Christian name Asa and thought I was doing him a favour.

Ashman thought differently.

'My name's 'Alan', he said, 'with one 'l'. Write it down.' And he swept on.

Asa Hartford, a midfielder, graduated to Albion's first team and made over two hundred appearances. He was supposed to move to Leeds United in 1971, but this transfer collapsed when he was found to have a hole in his heart. He did later have two spells with Manchester City and also played for Nottingham Forest, Everton and Norwich before he began a descent down the leagues. More importantly, he earned fifty caps playing for Scotland in the ten years from 1972 and was in the national squad for the 1978 and 1982 World Cups.

Hartford sought me out two weeks later at the next youth home game. He was only three years younger then me, shorter that I expected with a strong Clydeside accent.

'I hear the guv'ner bollocked youse because of my name,' he said.

'Yeah. I'm sorry Asa. I just got it wrong. I was trying to make a joke out of the fact that you scored two ace goals.'

'Hey, don't worry. It's my new nickname back hame. The family all make a point of saying 'Ace – er' very slowly. They're proud. I've kept the cutting.'

'No hard feelings, then.'

After finally moving as player / manager to Shrewsbury Town in 1989 where he played twenty-five games, Hartford went into caretaker and assistant management and coaching without great success. He looked after Manchester City's reserves team for several years, then a year at Blackpool before being sacked after less than a year at Macclesfield Town and then was made redundant after working the junior teams at Accrington Stanley.

Wherever Hartford went from there, a 2023 report stated his net worth at $5 million.

As for Ashman, West Bromwich Albion was impatient for further trophies and he was dismissed in 1971, hearing the news from a waiter while on holiday in Greece. He later managed Olympiakos before returning to Carlisle in 1971, leading the club into the First Division. From there, he dropped to Workington and Walsall before taking junior coaching roles.

# MICHAEL ANTONY ASTON

English archaeologist and *Time Team* star

# CHARLES NICHOLL

English author of history, biography and literary detection

*Mick Aston, 2007, centre, with Tony Robinson, left, and Guy de la Bédoyère on a Time Team shoot.* Bédoyère.

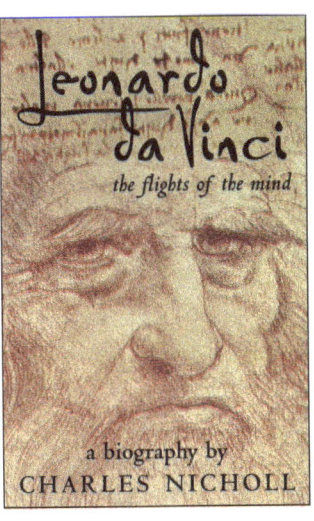

*Charles Nicholl, 2005.* Baillie Gifford Prize for Non-Fiction.

My PhD research into the felt hatting industry and a wish to share the results took me to all corners of the kingdom. I particularly valued the opportunity to meet the many village societies around Bristol where my work was concentrated. Local enthusiasm often surprised me. For the last two years of my degree, I was in such demand that I limited my performances to one a fortnight. Audiences of up to two hundred were not unusual.

One of the interesting by-products of giving talks is that one sometimes had to share the stage with other people and this double act may be illuminating. It also could be previously unmentioned and, therefore, with no preparation.

That's how I met Mick Aston, the resident academic on the Channel 4 television series *Time Team*, which ran from 1994 to 2011. Mick specialised in Early Medieval landscape archaeology and was a lecturer at the University of Bristol (where I studied) and at the University of Oxford.

He was a familiar sight with his tanned and bald dome surrounded by two sets of bushy grey hair which sparkled when the camera caught him against the sun. I attended a couple of his lectures at Bristol University, but had never met him. I did, however, warm to him because he was also an advocate of taking one's findings to the public. TV audiences loved him also; he was a necessary contrast to the *Time Team* presenter Tony Robinson. The regular conflict between the two was evident as Robinson majored on false tension and TV performance while Aston refused to budge on accuracy.

I went to the stage to set up and was surprised to find seating for five hundred.

'You'll keep it to an hour?' I was asked anxiously.

'I was told ninety minutes and that's what I've prepared,' I riposted, 'and that's without questions from the audience.'

'But Mick Aston's on straight after you at eight o'clock. We can't keep him waiting.' The lady's eyes were shining with excitement, if not adulation.

When you come up against the famous, you soon get put in your place. I was the warm up act and no one had bothered to tell me.

I didn't see the legendary Mick before it was time to get started. The hall was full. Tickets had all been sold and a lot of money gathered in. Not realising this, I had, as usual, forgone my fee and expenses.

'Thank you all for coming tonight to hear Mike Aston from *Time Team*. But, before we do, we have another speaker ...'

My talk was on trade unions in the early felt hat industry, a feisty subject with lots of strikes, violence and general bad humour. I abandoned my slide presentation, having no time to edit it and took to the stage wielding a hatter's bow I had recently made. The bow was six feet long and a fearsome tool.

I hammed it up and deliberately gave a less than academic performance. I played the parts of the strikers and manufactory owners, moving from one side of the stage to another, envisioning disputes and inventing behind-the-scenes arguments. I finished with the striking hatters defeated and figuratively laying on the floor around me. It was more one-man show than a mature exposition.

I came off to loud and prolonged clapping and demands for a longer session to allow questions. Some of the audience were standing.

In the wings, stood Mick.

'Bloody hell,' he said. 'This is unfair, you bastard. I'll never get them to listen to me.'

But he did. He was excellent. At the end we took two stools onto centre stage and fielded questions together. He was stylish enough to send a note commending me to my two supervisors at the university.

That same year, 2012, I gave another talk at the Chawton House library in Hampshire. The library is an internationally respected research and learning centre for the study of early women's writing from 1600 to 1830. For my visit, the rooms were out to hire. There was a more modest forty people in the audience for it was a different style of performance. University departments, this time History at Southampton, regularly put together events over a day or two which gave research students from across the country the opportunity to share their work before critical peers and lecturers. One had to apply in writing to get vetted and selected to present. These beauty parades were sometimes tense affairs as senior but insecure staff sought to display their credentials by belittling others. The events were, however, deemed a right of passage in getting work to doctoral standards.

I see from notes that my talk was called 'The Dog that Didn't Bark in the Night'. For the life of me, I can't recall what it was actually about, but it matters not. The subject was well received and did interest the one guest speaker. He sought me out and asked me to have dinner with him that evening to discuss it.

That's how I met the author, Charles Nicholl. As an historian, he may not be the most widely-known, but to me he was a literary hero and I was delighted. He has an unusual writing style, taking scraps of historical research that others might miss and poking them every which way to extract the fullest meaning and building a composite picture. His work on Shakespeare is, in my opinion, a masterpiece, and that on Da Vinci not far behind.[3] He has also written books on Thomas Nashe, Christopher Marlow and Arthur Rimbaud.

---

3 Nicholl, Charles, *Leonardo da Vinci: Flights of Mind* (2004) and *The Lodger: Shakespeare on Silver Street* (2007).

We spent a very pleasant evening in a cocoon among the other attendees which ended with him inviting me to visit his family and stay at his home near Lucca in Italy.

Sadly, I am not good at these things and never made it. It is something I regret.

# ODD INGOLF BAKKE

## Norwegian WWII resistance fighter

A man I didn't know came into my bedroom. I was astounded. As an eleven-year-old, no man, certainly not even my father, had ever come through my door. More shocking was that this stranger sat on my bed beside me and began casually to discuss my tens of carefully painted plastic model airplanes hanging by threads from drawing pins in the ceiling. He recognised them all, reeling off their names one after another. He spoke with a funny accent.

*Film poster for* The Heroes of Telemark. Columbia Pictures.

'Are you Auntie Freda's new boyfriend?' I asked.

'I am,' he replied with a laugh. 'My name's Ingolf, but I'll tell you a secret. It isn't my real first name.'

'What is it?'

'Well, it's a bit embarrassing. My first name is 'Odd', which is a normal name back in Norway where I come from, but everyone tells me that people in England will laugh at me if I use it. What do you think?'

I was being asked for an opinion. My world was turning upside down.

I told him I thought he had done the right thing. 'Odd' was a bit, well, odd.

'OK. That's what I'll do. Thanks. Why did you choose these planes?'

I explained that I was mad about planes. I cycled all over to the small airfields and to Heathrow near my home in Southall, Middlesex, to see them and to collect their numbers. I had a book that listed all the private plane numbers in the UK and underlined their entry when I spotted them.

'Can I see your book?'

This attention was stretching my credulity. No one ever displayed this sort of interest in my affairs. Ingolf studied my book in detail, asking several questions and listening to my answers.

'Mainly the planes on the ceiling are what I can afford,' I told him. 'They're generally smaller ones, like fighters and bombers. The really big ones cost a lot more money. How do you know their names? Are you a pilot?'

That would make Ingolf a God.

'No, but most of the planes are from the war, which was not so long ago. I saw them in Norway when we were fighting the Germans.'

He pointed to a model of the Focke-Wulf 190. 'I shot one of those down.'

I think my jaw hit the floor.

'How?'

'A friend of mine had just been killed. I was mad. I grabbed a machine gun and I was lucky. The plane flew into my bullets. It crashed into the ground near a shed in a big ball of fire. The pilot was killed. And our family cow.'

Auntie Freda, bubbling with pride at her latest beau, appeared at the door. She told us both to come down for tea so we went. There was tension in the house which I didn't understand. My attempts to explain Ingolf's knowledge and experiences were diverted. My father sat with a stony face which boded trouble for us for the rest of the week. His sulks always ended in punishments, but that was all I knew of how family life should be.

I learned later the cause of his mood. Ingolf was a war hero. My father was not. He had served, of course, but as a signaller and wireless operator. He had been in west Africa and Italy, even at Eisenhower's headquarters near Naples, but he had never fired a shot in anger. That meant my father was ashamed and, being the man he was, resented Ingolf despite him representing all that my father wished he could have been himself.

What made it worse was that Ingolf was an expert skier, a keen fisherman and a celebrated organist in his home near Oslo. These were manly skills. Ingolf had also lived in Sweden and Denmark and that meant he was an adventurer. My father didn't like leaving home. Ingolf first came to England in the previous year studying at the Tailor & Cutter Academy in London; he had also attended the *Norsk Tilsjaer Akedemi* for fashion design and pattern making.

This gave my father his opening. Any man interested in fashion was clearly a homosexual and not a suitable person to be around children. I was told never to allow him into my room again or dreadful things would happen.

Later, Ingolf became a member of the Export Council of Norway in Pall Mall, London. With Alfreda, in 1961, he started an agency for importing Norwegian sports wear and handicrafts. They married in 1965 after his previous marriage was dissolved.

A failed marriage proved everything my father believed about Ingolf. Born in 1907, he was also eleven years older than my aunt and, therefore, completely unsuitable.

Ingolf and Alfreda were married for six days over a year. He died, aged fifty-nine, of cerebral haemorrhage and heart failure. What we never fully understood was that Ingolf's early death was due to his war experiences and the damage suffered by his body. He was always on borrowed time.

The year before his death, Odd Ingolf Bakke and Alfreda went to see a recently-released war film, *The Heroes of Telemark*, an Anthony Mann production based on the sabotage of an Norwegian heavy water plant and starring Kirk Douglas, Richard Harris and Ulla Jacobsson.[4] That was when Ingolf's involvement came out.

Ingolf was never one of the named heroes who parachuted in to conduct the mission. He was one of the resistance fighters on the ground who helped to provide cover while the trained commandos went to work. Ingolf's side of the plan went wrong. There were a series of desperate gun battles, long chases and attacks by aircraft. He was forced into the mountains to escape capture and execution as happened to his comrades. He survived for over a year in a high cave in the snowy wilderness living on moss, lichen and a reindeer carcass, only occasionally supplemented by meagre food parcels delivered at great risk. He suffered serious heart damage and, when he finally got down to civilisation, spent a long time in convalescence.

The sabotage was aimed at the Vemork power station at the Rjukan waterfall in Telemark. The heavy water it produced was thought crucial to attempts to produce an atomic bomb which could have cost the Allies the war. Norwegian commandos eventually destroyed the production facility and this was followed by long and heavy Allied bombing raids to prevent repairs. The Germans attempted to move the remaining heavy water to Germany, but resistance forces sank the ferry carrying the water, *SF Hydro*, on Lake Tinn, killing eighteen

---

4  Haukelid, Knut, *Skis Against the Atom* (1954); Drummond, John, *But for These Men* (1962).

civilians. It was later found that the heavy water load was only a tenth of the minimum required for bomb construction.

My father continued to disparage Ingolf until his own death as an alcoholic in 1995.

# SHIRLEY VERONICA BASSEY
## Welsh singer

Shirley Bassey's career spans over seventy years in which she sold over one hundred and forty million records worldwide making her one of the best-selling female artists of all time. She was the first woman to claim a 'Top 40' album in seven consecutive decades in the United Kingdom. Surprisingly, despite winning most of the awards in her industry, including twenty-seven 'Top 40' hits in the UK, she achieved only two number ones: *As I Love You* and the double A-side *Climb Ev'ry Mountain* and *Reach for the Stars*.

*Shirley Bassey, 1973.* Mallet 100.

Born in Tiger Bay in the rough end of Cardiff in 1937 to a Nigerian father and English mother, Bassey had her first daughter when she was aged seventeen. She married twice: to Kenneth Hume in 1961 and to Sergio Novak in 1968; both ending in divorce. She was also well known for an affair with the actor Peter Finch. Her second daughter was found dead, aged twenty-one, in the River Avon in Bristol in 1985. Bassey declared it was not a suicide. However, in 2010, the police claimed that the convicted killer Michael Moffat was involved in the death. After the investigation, the police concluded that 'no criminal act was involved'.

Bassey became well-known internationally for being the only person to sing the theme songs for three James Bond films: *Goldfinger* (1964), *Diamonds Are Forever* (1971) and *Moonraker* (1979). She was made Dame Commander of the

Order of the British Empire (DBE) in 2000 and appointed, in 2024, a Member of the Order of the Companions of Honour (CH). She now lives in Monaco.

During the 1970s, I travelled regularly into London to watch professional boxing at the Royal Albert Hall. It was a golden era. The regulars are now all names of the past, but a few still hold a place in the pantheon: John L Gardner, Dave 'Boy' Green, Johnny Owen, Alan Minter, John H Stracey and Jim Watt. However, that is all another story.

Some time in this period, perhaps 1975, I noticed Shirley Bassey was in concert at the venue. To be honest, I was a little in love with her. It was several years since I had attended any musical events: the early Rolling Stones, Joe Brown, Dion, Duane Eddy, Gerry and the Pacemakers – you get the picture and, again, another story.

I read recently that Bassey's first Albert Hall concert was in 1971 and that she has appeared there forty-five times so what year she performed for me I cannot now say. At the end of a barnstorming night, I went to the stage door to see if I could catch a glimpse of her. I was a little late and there was no one there so I decided that I had missed her.

Then the door opened and there she was, a little flustered and all alone. The door slammed locked behind her. She let out a few rude words.

'Can I help you?' I asked.

She looked me up and down and replied, 'Can you believe it, I got lost and took the wrong turning. My manager and minders are inside somewhere and now I can't get back in.' There were a few more expletives. Her speaking voice was quite soft with an American-Welsh lilt, a shock after the power of her singing. She was beautiful.

'Would you like me to walk you round the building to find the right door?' I offered.

She looked me up and down again.

'Why are you standing here?'

'I guess I got the wrong door, too. I've been to your concert. You were great. I was hoping to get a sight of you a little closer than from the back of the hall.'

'OK. I guess I can trust you.' She slipped her arm in mine and we set off. We didn't say much. She was clearly distressed and I was overwhelmed.

About a quarter way round the building, walking down an ill-lit street, she suddenly brightened.

'There's my car and driver,' she pointed, 'but I can't see my manager.'

We got to the car and the driver, who had been looking in the other direction, jumped out and opened a rear door. He started to speak.

'Don't ask and don't wait for the others,' she told him. 'Take me straight to the hotel.'

Shirley Bassey freed her arm and turned to me.

'Thank you very much, kind sir. You saved me from a fate worse than death.'

She stood on tiptoe and pecked me swiftly on the cheek, turned quickly into the limousine, and was gone.

The cheek was the right one, the one that's unwashed.

# ALLAN ROBERT BORDER

## Australian cricket batsman and captain

Within a couple of hours of each other that Sunday in 1993, there were two unpleasant incidents with world-famous people and, in different ways, I had to deal with both of them.

It was a typical May day for English cricket, overcast, threatening rain, time for woolly scarves and, occasionally, a chink of pale sun. Somerset was shortly to start the second of three days' play against the Australians at Taunton. The Australia side was to declare at its overnight score of 431 for seven in which Michael Slater had scored 122.

*Allan Border, 2014.* Australian Embassy in India.

Our party of three stayed at *The Castle Hotel* and met for a late breakfast. Midway through the cereal, we heard a loud argument from the feature table in the bay window where two guests were in spiteful debate. I say 'debate', but, in truth, this wasn't a two-way conversation. The male of the pair was laying into his partner with a gusto that reached every table in the room.

It was then that we realised that the man was one of the most recognisable comedians and actors in the UK and anywhere else which took British comedy series. The woman was his wife – 'I have no idea why I married you. You are the thickest person on earth.'

She looked very nice and bit her proverbial tongue as the stream of abuse landed. He looked like a monster. There was no thought of lowering his tone.

He didn't care. He even might have enjoyed the twenty other diners hearing every word.

I've not named him, but I would dearly like to. This had a potential fight followed by a court case written all over it, even today. I had no doubt his screen success had brought him wealth.

The root of the matter was the lady's inability to provide sufficient insights into the *Sunday Telegraph*'s general knowledge crossword of which our hero considered himself an undoubted master.

We three agreed to meet later in the day at the Taunton Brewhouse Art Gallery where my aunt, Alfreda Bakke, a sculptress of some local renown, had a number of exhibits. We were to meet her there and provide moral support. Two of us then set out for the county cricket ground.

We huddled into our seats. There were few people watching the game, delayed by a damp pitch, even though it was the Australian tourists. It turned colder and everyone seemed a little miserable as they waited for more rain that would ruin the day. Even the beer seemed flat. Somerset lost two quick wickets and the crowd, all fifty of us, was a little boisterous if only to keep warm. Andy Hayhurst and Chris Tavaré were batting. This is the same Hayhurst who, in 2015, was jailed for two years for stealing over £100,000 by fraud from a cricket club.

Standing near the boundary, yet to bowl, was the Australian sensation-to-be, leg break bowler Shane Warne. Warne was about to be catapulted to cricketing fame by bowling the 'Ball of the Century' against experienced English batsman Mike Gatting. Warne ended this, his first Ashes series, leading all bowlers with thirty-four wickets at an average of 25.79. Warne went on to revolutionise cricket thinking. He died in 2022, aged fifty-two, of a heart attack while holidaying in Thailand.

There was another side to Warne, one that the English were keen to play up. The first thing was that at that time he was a little overweight, not badly, but under a couple of cricket jumpers in the Taunton outfield, he looked particularly so. The Press and spectators had taken to calling him 'Tubby Warne' in order to get a rise from him and they were having some success. During his career, especially later, Warne was involved in off-field scandals including a ban from cricket for testing positive for a prohibited substance, a colourful personal life, interactions with gambling figures and thinning hair which he had artificially replaced and advertised widely.

On this cold day at Taunton with not a lot happening on the field, the insults began to flow as Warne patrolled the boundary. It obviously got to him and he became visibly upset. Of course, that only made it worse. Soon the small section of the crown around me joined in.

Warne made his way over to his captain, the legendary Allan Border.

Border was one of the greatest cricketers of all time. He eventually played 156 Test matches, at that time a record, hitting twenty-seven centuries. He retired as Australia's most-capped player and leading run scorer in both Tests and One-Day Internationals. He went on to become a top cricket commentator.

The sight of Border comforting the poor lamb, Warne, was a delight to the crowd. Border rounded on the barrackers who were spread across many rows. He told them, generally, that they were an *expletive* disgrace. This was no way to treat an *expletive* guest to their *expletive* country. Their comments were *expletive* hurtful and harmful. He had a good mind to come into the crowd and give someone an *expletive* doing.

Then I had my 'personal moment'. Border came right to the fence close to where I was sitting and chose me for his anger. I swear to you, I had said nothing nor shouted any disparagement. That sort of thing is not my style. I did raise my beer can to him in salute. And, shame to tell, I had been enjoying it all.

But that didn't stop Border.

'And you,' he said, pointing at me and shaking with anger, 'you *short expletive*, I'm going to have you thrown out for all your *expletive* rudeness or we will all leave this *expletive* pitch and never come back to this *expletive* place.'

With that, he turned and strode off to talk to the umpires, David Shepherd and Ken Palmer, and then marched to the pavilion, while his players gathered around Warne near the pitch, consoling him.

Nothing much happened for five minutes until two elderly groundsmen worked their way over to our part of the stands.

'Where's the chap that had a barney with Border?' asked one.

'He left,' someone replied. 'He was upset by Border's language. He's gone to make a complaint. He wants Border thrown out.'

The match resumed. Somerset made 151-4. Warne took a wicket and the rain came down. We all went off to the bar. Next day, after a couple of quick declarations, Australia bowled Somerset out for 285 and won the match by a handful of runs. Warne took four wickets.

Personally, I think the confrontation meant that England lost the six Test Ashes series that day. Australia won 4-1. It was Warne's breakthrough year and he got riled in Taunton.

I didn't need counselling for all the unpleasant things that had happened to me, an innocent bystander, possibly because Auntie Freda sold all four of her exhibits and was well praised and, therefore, pleased.

# ROELOF FREDERIK 'PIK' BOTHA

South African Minister of Foreign Affairs

# JEREMY BERNARD CORBYN

Leader of the Labour Party and the UK's Opposition

# JOHN ENOCH POWELL

British politician, scholar and writer

*Pik Botha, 1981.* Ronald Regan Presidential Library.

*Jeremy Corbyn, 2024.* Jessica Taylor, Parliamentary Archives.

*Enoch Powell, 1987.* Allan Warren.

Three dissimilar politicians from different eras, Pik Botha, the South African foreign affairs minister in the time of apartheid, Jeremy Corbyn, far-left Labour leader from 2015 to 2020 and possible UK prime minister, and Enoch Powell, right-wing intellectual in government in the 1960s, were all *Marmite*.

Their flock loved them; their opponents hated them for supposed extremism. From my point of view, they were also all notable orators. They had the skill of moving audiences to something close to adulation or anger. Only Nigel Farage, today, carries that same ability to inspire the common man and to distress the chattering classes. Elsewhere, the skills of public speaking rest in the hands of the professionally dull and the grey.

That's why I went out of my way to attend speeches by all three men. It was not a question of agreement, but of a great interest in the art. Unexpectedly, on each occasion, I was selected from the crowd to ask a question and those interventions gave me three more personal moments with the famous.

Botha was nicknamed Pik, short for *pikkewyn*, Afrikaans for 'penguin', because of his physical stance, especially when wearing a suit. He was the soft face of P W Botha's National Party, a recognised liberal, friendly and conciliatory to the outside world. Although a failed leadership candidate, and no blood relation to the prime minister, he remained in office for eleven years.

On Nelson Mandela's release and taking power in 1994, Pik Botha served under him as Minister of Mineral and Energy Affairs until 1996. He was one of the few members of the old government to repent his involvement in apartheid which, by the 1970s, he said, he had realised was 'morally wrong' and he did not do enough to 'turn the tide' and to prevent atrocities.

South Africa held a parliamentary election in 1984 which was when I went to hear Botha talk in a large secondary school hall in Randburg, north-west of Johannesburg. Botha was not on home ground. The satellite city was relatively liberal and elected Democratic Party members. However, in the hall, you wouldn't have known it. It was packed. Botha was preaching to the faithful; the audience was predominately Afrikaners and I felt a tad unsettled. He began and ended in their language, switching to English in the middle. His style that day was confrontational, punchy with many one-liners and insider jokes. It was easy to see his influence. While disagreeing with much of what he said, I was impressed with how he said it.

At the door on entry, there were tear off sheets of paper on which to write questions alongside one's name. This would allow the ultra-conservative party worthies to pick the subjects; there was to be no face to face debate.

With no prior thought, I wrote asking Botha why he had come to Randburg when he had no chance of winning. To my great surprise, after about five questions, all in Afrikaans, my name was called. I stood as requested and repeated what I had written. There was a little gasp.

'No,' said Botha (as best as I can remember). 'Don't upset this English speaker. He's even got a red neck.' This was a little local joke: *rooi*, 'red', and *nek*, 'neck' was the Afrikaner term for South Africans of British descent who went hatless and didn't protect their necks from sunburn. 'It's a good question. I admit it would be unusual to win in Randburg, but I am a politician and a politician for all the people. Change may be coming and I want everyone to have a chance to see me and to hear my point of view, no matter which way they vote.'

A day later, at work, my manager said out of nowhere that he was pleased that I was taking an interest in local politics, but as a foreigner on a work pass I should not get too publicly involved.

Botha died in 2018 at his home in Pretoria, aged eighty-six.

People feel freer today to disparage Jeremy Corbyn now he is out of real power, but his influence behind the scenes among the left of the left remains high. He is still a member of the Socialist Campaign Group parliamentary caucus. In his heyday, he was one step away from being prime minister. Keir Starmer voted for Corbyn's leadership and current deputy prime minister Angela Rayner is an avowed supporter.

Corbyn began politics as a trade unionist active in Haringey, Hornsey and Islington. He has consistently and publicly nailed his flag to the same causes: anti-fascism, anti-apartheid, the Campaign for Nuclear Disarmament, a smaller military which would stay at home, against the Vietnam, Iraq and Afghanistan wars, for renationalisation of public utilities and railways, for large increases in welfare spending, anti-Brexit, and for a united Ireland and Palestinian statehood. The Metropolitan Police Special Branch monitored Corbyn for twenty years until the early 2000s as he was 'deemed to be a subversive'.

As a backbencher, he often voted against the Labour whip. He received the Ghandi International Peace Award and the Seán MacBride Peace Prize. When Ed Miliband lost the 2015 general election, Corbyn won the vote to succeed him as leader of the Labour Party. He became wildly popular among a section of the party, increasing the share of the vote by ten per cent in the 2017 election.

I got to question Corbyn by chance in 2015. I had arranged with one of my doctoral supervisors, Richard Sheldon, at Bristol University, to meet him and his family at the annual Tolpuddle Martyrs' Festival in Dorset. In the end, he didn't make it and I was free to wander among the thousands of people and listen to the many events celebrating trade unionism.

At Tolpuddle in 1834, the government conspired to ruin a legal trade union by making it illegal for workmen to combine for trade purposes.[5] Strikers were charged with making secret oaths, defying an act passed specifically to deal with a naval mutiny. Spies were planted and six leading trade unionist were arrested, five of whom were Wesleyan preachers. A trial was hurried forward before a picked jury and a hostile judge. The six men were sentenced to seven years' transportation and sent chained and manacled to Portsmouth. Two years later, after considerable public outcry, they were all granted a free pardon but were kept in New South Wales, Australia, by subterfuge for another two years.

Corbyn fever was high at Tolpuddle. The chant, 'Jeremy, Jeremy Corbyn' was regularly taken up in meetings. Knickknacks carrying his name were for sale everywhere.

I attended a talk titled 'What would the Tolpuddle Martyrs make of Farming today?' Towards the end of a damning indictment, Corbyn was noticed in the crowd. He was invited to the stage and questions were asked. There were a couple of obsequious comments and then a pause. I stood up. It was not long since the Conservative party leadership had been bombed by the Provisional IRA at a Brighton Hotel, leaving five dead with thirty injured.

'In retrospect,' I asked, 'do you regret asking the Sinn Féin leader Gerry Adams, two convicted IRA volunteers and other members of that party to Westminster two weeks after the bombing?'

There was some unpleasant catcalling and booing at the question, but Corbyn was not fazed. He always stood by the side of the Irish republicans against the Protestants of the north.

'No, I don't regret it,' he replied. 'Dialogue is needed in the hardest of times. I will always argue for peace.'

I got plenty of glares when I later left the tent. In 2017, Corbyn said he had 'never met the IRA', which was later clarified to admitting that he had met them 'but it was in their capacity as activists for Sinn Féin'.

All round, the day was most enjoyable. I was staying at a B&B in the village of Sandford Orcas near Sherborne. That evening, at the local pub for dinner, I gave the manager a package of beer mats emblazoned with Corbyn's name.

---

5   Heal, Chris, *Ropley's Legacy* (C&S 2021), pp. 187-8.

'Who he?' he asked.

'Remember you heard it here first,' I said. The mats were soon snapped up.

Enoch Powell will forever be notorious and blasphemed for his 'Rivers of Blood' speech in Birmingham in 1968 in which he criticised rapid immigration to the UK from the Commonwealth. He was fired from the shadow cabinet the day afterwards by Edward Heath, the Conservative leader of the opposition.

Powell was a classical scholar and brigadier who had served in the second world war. His defining speech contained an allusion to the Roman poet Virgil:

> *I am filled with foreboding. Like the Roman, I seem to see 'the River Tiber foaming with much blood'. That tragic and intractable phenomenon which we watch with horror on the other side of the Atlantic but which there is interwoven with the history and existence of the States itself, is coming upon us here by our own volition and our own neglect. Indeed, it has all but come. In numerical terms, it will be of American proportions long before the end of the twentieth century. Only resolute and urgent action will avert it even now. Whether there will be the public will to demand and obtain that action I do not know. All I know is that to see, and not to speak, would be a great betrayal.*

Overnight, Powell became the most popular politician in Britain. Polls suggested that sixty-seven to eighty-two per cent of the population agreed with him. There was a street demonstration in his support by a thousand dockers. Meat porters from Smithfield Market handed in a ninety-two page petition. And, yet, the left-wing establishment sought to cancel him and largely succeeded. To mention his name, even today, is to receive an automatic charge of racialism. It was the beginning of a great divide that continues without resolution between the establishment's commitment to multiculturalism and the importation of cheap labour and with the views of the great mass of the electorate on restricting immigration.

So, I found myself, a young journalist, in Wolverhampton to hear Powell's follow-up speech. It was heaving. I only got inside because of my press card and a few of us were given privileged seating at the side of the hall by the stage. If I hadn't been that close to the microphones, I would never have heard a word. Powell was screamed down, particularly by the Socialist Workers Party who had turned out in force and were well-organised with banners and megaphones.

Powell's message was not to be allowed. I saw hysterical young people out of control, some fainting with emotion.

After half an hour, the organisers gave up and Powell was hustled out of the room under guard. After a few minutes, we journalists were asked if we would like to join him in an anteroom. I asked the obvious question:

'Given the result we have seen tonight, do you regret your choice of language and timing, which you say yourself was considered and deliberate? Have you moved the argument?'

I don't recall Powell's reply word for word. What he said in his measured tones was that free speech was at stake. The lunatic left sought to kill debate and he saw this trend extending into politics and into universities. The answer to my question was in his original speech, 'to see, and not to speak, would be a great betrayal'.

Enoch Powell died in 1998 in a London hospital. He asked where his lunch was and was told he was being fed intravenously. His last remark was, 'I don't call that much of a lunch.' He was buried in his brigadier's uniform at his regiment's plot in Warwick.

# JAMES GORDON BROWN

## Scottish UK Prime Minister

Having sat at my keyboard for half an hour, idly punching in sentence starts then deleting them, I realised that I don't want to write about Gordon Brown. Flicking through the names on my list of seventy special moments with the famous, I can easily cast Brown very near the bottom in terms of those with whom I would like to spend any social time. I well understand that this will horrify his many admirers who see him as a great and compassionate leader. Not me, I'm afraid.

*Gordon Brown, c. 2008.* National Archives.

Despite all the upfront machismo, I found him arrogant, defensive, tense, sullen, humourless and deeply boring. His family probably see him as a giant teddy bear.

Brown was born in Giffnock, Scotland, in 1951, a 'son of the manse'. He took a doctorate at Edinburgh University which took over ten years to complete on 'The Labour Party and Political Change in Scotland 1918-1929'. He was a college lecturer and then tutor at the Open University. He later worked as a journalist at Scottish Television, graduating to current affairs. There was little here to suggest an international outlook or the economics background that would lead him to be the UK's longest serving and, some would say, most successful and daringly reforming chancellor of the exchequer.

At a, perhaps, apocryphal restaurant meeting, Brown agreed not to stand against Tony Blair, the rising and charismatic star, in return for the chancellorship and control of UK policy. This happened in 1997 and Brown lasted over ten years in the job while dealing with an increasingly fractious relationship with Blair that finally bubbled over into open hostility. Brown's temper at the time was public and legendary.

When Blair stepped down, Brown was elected unopposed as leader of the Labour Party and became Prime Minister in 2007. In 2010, Brown stood down and the resulting hung parliament led to a Conservative Liberal Democrat coalition. Brown retired to the back benches as MP for Kirkcaldy and Cowdenbeath.

Since 2012, Brown has served as UN Special Envoy for Global Education and was appointed as World Health Organisation Ambassador for Global Health Financing in 2021.

About 2006, before Brown's premiership, I had a share in an internet startup looking at automating large parts of an accountant's business. The most important part of the endeavour was producing the backroom software which I left to others. One aspect I took to myself was to raise the company's profile, and gain seed funding, by entering the business into the many awards for industry that were available at the time. You may well know the sort of thing: 'The Young Business of the Year', 'The Most Innovative Newcomer', 'The New Business Most Likely to Succeed', etc, etc.

I entered our business in ten of these and reached the long shortlist in eight. It was the award season and successful applicants were invited to pay for a moderate dinner at a high price in a London West End hotel. There was always a comedian compère and the better newspapers and business organisations that ran these affairs usually pulled in a big name as guest speaker.

Sadly for me, on three of these occasions, that speaker was Gordon Brown and each time he gave the same speech. By the third time, I was able to parrot his lines, and his mediocre jokes, before he made them which seriously upset one table member and Labour Party devotee.

Some of his hubris was hard to believe. It was without shame or apparent irony. Every sentence started with 'I'. 'I am the longest serving chancellor with the best record … I personally have ended the era of boom and bust … I have led the greatest resurgence in the British economy … I have not been frightened to change this or that … I have not been slow to give the Bank of England operational independence ...I have improved living conditions for every working person in the UK ... I have led the fight for the poor and underprivileged.'

Even diehards shifted uncomfortably in their seats. Some of his pronouncements were downright untrue and others illusory. He tried to radiate truth, power, belief, but the more he continued the more shallow it all sounded.

On the third occasion as he finished he was asked to tour the room and shake some paws. At my table were a couple of business leaders who were known to him. By chance the seat next to me was empty, its occupant having gone to the toilet, perhaps to vomit. Brown sat down.

I asked him about the reasons for the sale of sixty per cent of the country's gold reserves at a knock down price, Gold had soared in value shortly afterwards in a bull market. Some estimates today suggested that Brown lost the UK some £23 billion.

I witnessed at first hand the legendary glower, then the politician kicked in. He gave a large chunk of his speech again, spittle flying, and never mentioned the gold. People stayed at the table out of politeness. At an appropriate place in the script, he got up and left without a personal word. There was a stunned silence.

'There goes a reputation,' said one victim.

My internet business got to the last six in all the eight entries and was runner up in three. We never won the big prize, but did gain some useful and profitable publicity. Sadly, the business eventually failed for a whole set of other reasons and I lost a good chunk of money.

# JAMES BURKE

Broadcaster, science historian, author

# SIR LUDOVIK HENRY COVERLEY KENNEDY

Scottish journalist and author

*James Burke, 2007.* Andrea Mann, Flickr.    *Ludo Kennedy.* The Independent.

In their days, James Burke and Ludovic Kennedy, seventeen years the senior, were stalwarts of British television screens. Both were English graduates at Oxford, broadcasters and authors, urbane and widely travelled, but their fields were different.

Burke was a science historian and one of the main presenters of the BBC1 series *Tomorrow's World* from 1965 to 1971. He created and presented the television series *Connection* in 1978 and its more philosophical sequel *The Day the Universe Changed* in 1985. In 1973, Burke predicted the widespread use of computers for business decisions, the creation of data banks of personal information, and changes in human behaviour, such as a greater willingness to reveal personal information to strangers. The *Washington Post* called him 'one of the most intriguing minds in the western world'. Burke was about bringing science to the people; making the complex understandable without talking down.

Kennedy was known for his work in current affairs. He was a reader of ITV's flagship *Independent Television News* alongside Robin Day and Chris Chataway. He presented the BBC's *Panorama* for many years. As an investigative journalist, he re-examined cases such as the Lindbergh kidnapping and many murder convictions, like those of of Timothy Evans and Derek Bentley. He also campaigned for the abolition of the death penalty in the United Kingdom, but supported assisted dying, standing for parliament as a Liberal on both these issues. Some of his books were turned into films, including *10 Rillington Place*, starring Richard Attenborough as serial killer Richard Christie. Other books included the atheistic statement *All in the Mind: A Farewell to God* in 1999. He married the actress and dancer Moira Shearer.

The two men did have one other characteristic in common. They were both broadcasters for hire and it was through their employment in separate projects with IBM in the UK that I got to work with them.

My manager at the time was in charge of employee communications. He was not greatly respected by his managerial peers or his staff and, within the company, was essentially friendless. He thought his position meant that his opinions, on religion, politics or, even, sport, were necessarily superior. If crossed, he would have tantrums during which he would lock himself in his office for the rest of the day. What he did possess in abundance was the energy to pursue his latest idea. In this case, the idea was to use video to communicate complex messages to the company at large. He felt the written word belonged to a previous generation. Paper had lost its power to persuade. He gathered a large budget and set about creating a television studio from which would emanate news programmes.

The first single subject programme produced was to announce complex changes in the company pension scheme. There was to be no dreary static face to camera in this whirlwind production, but a living set full of colour, visual aids and moving parts with a presenter, himself, gliding seamlessly between the props. He would also direct. Errors from his inexperienced staff were met with towering rages. The closer it got to a recording deadline, the more he acquired television characteristics and imagined language. Some of it was beyond parody.

In all truth, the set was brilliant and did the job of simplifying and explaining. What didn't work was his performance. There came the day when he was forced to admit that we had all let him down and therefore he couldn't be the on camera lead.

Someone suggested hiring in the talent and James Burke was approached at short notice. Luckily, he was available at a suitable fee, but had little time for rehearsal. For him, it was an in and out job.

'Can I have the script?' Burke asked at our morning briefing meeting.

There was an embarrassed silence. There never had been a script. It had always been about performance.

'Why haven't you got the script ready?' I was asked.

I could see Burke was on the cusp of walking out.

'I'll deliver it to your home early this evening,' I offered him.

I finished the work in time, but my manager insisted on taking it home with him to 'correct'. He was livid that I had met the deadline. I was left to apologise to Burke.

The script came back to me next morning, I think with three extra commas, a corrected spelling mistake and an inserted sentence. It was now 'just usable'.

Burke arrived, told me in a few words that he understood exactly what had gone on, thanked me and asked for a room and half-hourly coffee. I saw the genius of a live performer. Three hours later, he came out, gave me back the script with a 'well done', indicated a couple of likely changes which he would handle on the hoof and then went out before an employee audience and gave a word perfect interactive live one-take, one-hour show that left me gasping in admiration.

A few years later, IBM in the UK, a fervent non-organised company from its American origins and ownership, was under attack from the trade unions. Because of the state of the current UK legislation, it was decided to allow all employees a vote on the matter. As part of IBM's presentation of its side of the argument, the company would produce a special 'for and against' copy of the company newspaper and a video in which employees would watch a synopsis of the options and then be free to ask questions of the directors. We were excruciatingly proud of our 'balance'.

I had to write the material. Ludovic Kennedy was felt to have the gravitas and acumen to be the interrogator-in-chief and I provided him with my work. He was charming, interested and thoroughly professional. He worked the recording like the expert he was.

The vote on unionisation was a walkover for the company. From memory, the count was over ninety per cent in IBM's favour on an over eighty per cent response.

# MANGOSUTHU GATSHA BUTHELEZI
## Zulu prince, KwaZulu Chief Minister

*Mangosuthu Buthelezi.*

Back in the dog days of legal apartheid in South Africa, the joke was that three Bothas ran the country: P W Botha, prime minister; Pik Botha, foreign minister; and Mangosuthu Buthelezi, Zulu president of the Inkatha Freedom Party (IFP).

Buthelezi was indeed one of the most prominent black politicians of the apartheid era. He was the chief minister and sole political leader of the KwaZulu Bantustan government and founded the IFP in 1975. It was his own personal fiefdom and a continuing thorn in the side of both the ruling National Party and the African National Congress. Post-apartheid, he was appointed minister of home affairs by Nelson Mandela for ten years to 2004.

He was also a Zulu prince and served as the traditional prime minister to the Zulu royal family from 1954 until his death two years ago in 2023. He was first appointed by King Goodwill Zwelithini Bhekuzuhu, the son of his uncle King Solomon kaDinuzulu. In turn, Dinuzulu was a son of King Cetshwayo who was the Zulu commander-in-chief during the Anglo-Zulu war of 1879 and responsible for the famous battles at Isandlwana and Rorke's Drift before final defeat at Ulundi. Despite partial film depictions, Cetshwayo consistently sought to make peace with the British, particularly Lord Chelmsford, who treated him badly.

Buthelezi played Cetshwayo in the film *Zulu* of 1964, which starred Stanley Baxter and Michael Caine in his first major film role. The battle of Isandlwana was described in the film *Zulu Dawn*, starring Burt Lancaster and Peter O'Toole in 1979.

In 1984, I sat down for lunch in a well-tended garden setting. I have to be honest, I can't be sure where it was. I know I had driven from Durban and think it likely it was among the soft Zulu *rondavel*-laden hills off the main road to Pietermaritzburg. I remember it as the garden to a residential house, standing alone, not in a *kraal*, so probably the modern home of a Zulu dignitary. I remember why I was there. Earlier, there had been a discreet event in which an IBM contribution to some *KwaZulu* infrastructure was received and recognised. Local Press were invited to meet some of the important guests and I was there to supervise them and their questions. The event had a topical importance because the local IBM subsidiary was keen to show its paymasters in the US that the company was well-thought of among the indigenous populations. American disinvestment hung thickly in the air and was a subject for regular government debate. Nerves were twitching. At this distance, I cannot for sure even remember the nature of the infrastructure, but I believe it was a specialist secondary school.

The few Press left early, placid and more that happy with the copious notes and photographs provided for them, as well as a bag of sandwiches and a couple of cans. A few words from the King and they were off. My own director had gone off, too, as well as King Goodwill and many of his entourage.

The event just seemed to fizzle out. The table was groaning with food. Several flunkies hovered. A colleague had settled at the far end of the table with some young Zulu men dressed as warriors and a party was in the making.

I called for a cold beer, picked up a beef rib and settled down in the shade. After a few minutes, a gentleman sat next to me.

'Mind if I join you?'

'Not at all. Excuse the fingers,' I said, waving the rib as delicately as I could. 'This looks your spread anyway so the 'thank you' is all mine.' I introduced myself.

'Pleasure. Tuck in. I think I'll join you.'

I now realised that I was sitting next to one of the most powerful men in South Africa, Mangosuthu Buthelezi. He was born in 1928, so almost twenty years my senior, but he looked a lot younger and very dapper in a made-to-measure suit.

'Need to watch the diabetes,' he said, 'but I will have a beer. The doctors have just discovered it and it's proving a right pain. I'm having to learn self control, but that's difficult for a dictator.'

Buthelezi was joking about his reputation. His administration was often described by his political enemies as a 'de facto one party state, intolerant of political opposition and dominated by the IFP.' Opposition rallies often burst into fatal violence.

I asked if he knew where everyone had gone.

'I do know your director is sick and has gone to lie down. Many of the king's advisers are getting on so they have also sought their beds. Don't let it worry you. As I said, tuck in. I'm sure we'll find something to talk about although I would quite like to give politics a rest as it seems like I have the afternoon off.'

I asked more about the diabetes (he was Type 2), of course not suspecting that I would be diagnosed with the same disease twenty years later.

He discovered I was a rugby fan and asked what I thought of the Springbok team just picked to play a covert international series. He particularly asked if I had seen any good emerging black players as I watched the provincial sides. We discussed tactics. He was knowledgeable.

To keep the mood light, I mentioned his role in playing his grandfather in the film *Zulu*.

'Hated it,' he said, 'standing around for hours', but he had done it so as to make sure that all the extras, Cetshwayo's army, got paid good daily rates. 'Didn't like seeing them get killed though.' He never met the principal actors, Caine or Baxter, but spent all his time looking regal standing on hilltops.

Buthelezi was educated at a famous mission school in Amanzimtoti and during the last years of the second war at the University of Fort Hare in the eastern Cape Province. I don't know what he studied, but we quickly got onto James Joyce, his all-time favourite. I explained I was still struggling with *Ulysees*. His favourites were *Dubliners* and *A Portrait of the Artist as a Young Man*. On a recent trip to London, he had slipped away for a few days to visit Dublin and had visited many of Joyce's haunts.

And so we spent a pleasant few hours away from the cares of the world. Eventually, one of his aides turned up and suggested he be elsewhere. We shook hands and thanked each other for the company. I collected my colleague and we together drove back to Durban.

# WILLIAM HENRY CHATTAWAY
English sculptor who lived in Paris

# DEBORAH GARMAN
Child of the Bloomsbury Set & the UK Communist Party

*Bill Chattaway.*  *Debbie Garman, left, with her father, Douglas.*

William Chattaway and Deborah Garman come from close to home: Uncle Bill was my wife's, Diane's, uncle, her father's younger brother, and Auntie Debbie, was Bill's wife. I have placed them together for this book, but they are individually famous for very different reasons. Both were regular visitors to our home in Hampshire and we to theirs in Paris.

Bill, born in 1927, spent most of the war at the Coventry School of Art and Design and then three years at the Slade School of Fine Art in London. He left for Paris in 1950 in the hope of finding the famous pre-war artistic centre of the Latin Quarter still bubbling with creative energy. Times had moved on for Paris and its Left Bank, but Bill found just enough encouragement to stay, living in a small flat in the narrow Rue Rousselet, parallel with the Boulevard des Invalides and home over the years to many artists, and with a separate studio within walking distance. He married Debbie in 1959. Much of the time, especially in the early days, life was hard, a hand to mouth existence with a son in tiny rooms on an upper floor of a tenement with no lift.

Bill became a successful and renowned sculptor with several important mentors and supportive galleries. He was heavily influenced by the Swiss Alberto Giacometti's *Walking Man* and by the sculptor's experiments with the human figure. Bill worked, particularly, with the female form as he looked for new spatial relationships and concepts of movement.

Over the years, we spent a number of evenings over a bottle of red wine while I tried to understand his motivation. He was always kindly, modest about his achievements and keen not to offend, but perhaps too trusting of those who made money from him in the Parisian art market. To take one of his plaster models, which which his studio was littered, laboriously crafted and re-crafted, trashed and begun again, and then guide it through a foundry to its final bronze state, was a process of deep determination. Here, perhaps, his greatest flaw lay, a necessary fault shared with most driven artists, a complete concentration on his work that vacillated between selfishness and other worldliness.

What personal moments to choose?

One summer, I was driving with my family to holiday in Italy. The new car, a Renault 25, regularly broke down. It was a holiday weekend and all garages seemed closed. Bill took up the case and harangued a man on the phone for what seemed hours in a search for a mechanic. 'But this is a vingt-cinque! The honour of France is at stake! What will the English say?'

Finally, he put the phone down and I asked, Success? Will he fix it?'

'No', said Bill. 'He was just the car park attendant.'

Bill's great quest at one time was to reduce the number of lines and curves in a new piece to the smallest number. He wanted to capture the essence in as few movements as possible. Our discussion turned to argument and lasted many hours.

In desperation, I said, 'But, what you are saying is that you want to reduce this pig (he was sculpting a sow) to just one straight line.'

'Yes,' he shouted. 'Now you've finally got it.'

Bill never received the financial independence he hoped for. A major sale was always a great relief. However, that is not to say he was not successful. I count almost a hundred exhibitions in Paris, London and New York and in and around his home town of Coventry. He has works in France in the Centre Georges Pompidou, and the Modern Art, Beauvais and Mont-de-Marsan Museums, in the UK in the British Museum and several universities and in the Hirshhorn Museum in Washington DC. His ordered work includes busts of François-René de Chateaubriand, Albert Einstein, Bertrand Russell, Charles Fourier and George Bernanos.

Bill died in 2019.

Deborah Garman might be famous enough for her translation of the Beatrix Potter children's novels into French. But, for me, she will always be best known, not so much for what she did, although she was a resourceful and surprising cook, as for the environment into which she was born and in which she grew up. As a child and young lady, the catalogue of visitors to her home and others who she knew is a *Who's Who* of contemporary UK artistic and left-wing political circles.[6]

Debbie's father was Douglas Garman, leading light with seven sisters of the bohemian and notorious Bloomsbury Set and long-standing and senior member of the British Communist Party. Garman was born into money and studied Classics, switching to English Literature, at Caius College, Cambridge, and 'seems to have acquired sympathies with the Communist Party there'. He spent the 1920s between London and Paris, and was teaching in Leningrad in 1926. With Edgell Rickword, he edited and wrote for a journal, *The Calendar of Modern Letters*, which briefly appeared in 1925 as a monthly literary review. He published a book of poems, *The Jaded Hero*, in 1927. He worked through the 1930s for the Marxist publishing house, Lawrence and Wishart, in London. Garman was Education Organiser of the Communist Party from 1934 to 1947. He ran summer schools at Swanage and was involved in the South Wales Hunger March of 1936, which he reported on behalf of the *Daily Worker*. He

---

6  Connolly, Cressida, *The Rare and the Beautiful* (Harper 2005).

also toured the country, trying to recruit for the International Brigade in the Spanish Civil War.

Garman's lived with his first wife, Jeanne Sophie Hewitt, in a flat in Bloomsbury and, later in Penybont, Wales. Their only child, Deborah, Debbie, was born in 1926. Jeanne had an affair with Garman's sister, Mary, and Garman became one of the lovers of the wealthy art collector and bohemian *bon vivant* Peggy Guggenheim. Garman and Guggenheim set up home in Yew Tree Cottage in South Harting, near Chichester. In 1936, it was agreed that Jeanne would look after Debbie in term time, but that she would stay with Garman and Guggenheim in South Harting during holidays.[7]

I drove Bill and Debbie one summer's day to Yew Tree Cottage, the first time Debbie had been back for fifty years. This would be my 'personal moment' with her. I offered to call in and see if the current occupants would allow a brief visit. Debbie declined as she 'wanted to remember it the way it was'.

'I loved Debbie,' wrote Guggenheim. 'She was just the opposite of any child I have ever known. She was so mature, calm, sensible, self contained and well behaved, and so little trouble. She was intellectual like her father.' There was also the benefit of Guggenheim's own daughter, Pegeen, of the same age. They were 'like sisters'.

Djuna Barnes, Ernest Wishart, Edgell Rickword, Bertrand Russell, Lewis Jones, Mavis Llewellyn, William Gerhardi and Samuel Beckett were among the many who visited Yew Tree Cottage and, by inference, Debbie.

Garman broke with Guggenheim and married Jessie Ayriss, the wife of a leading Communist Party member. Much later, he retired to a farm in Dorset, where he continued to write, including the *Shell Guides to England*. It was there that Diane, as a young girl, visited him. Garman remained a member of the Communist Party until his death in 1969.

Of Garman's sisters, Mary married the fascist South African poet, Roy Campbell, and had affairs with Jeanne Hewitt and with the writer, Vita Sackville-West, who, in turn had an affair with Arabian hero, T E Lawrence. Kathleen had three children by Sir Jacob Epstein, the sculptor, and then married him. Epstein's jealous wife, Margaret, shot and wounded Kathleen and encouraged her husband into multiple affairs in the hope that Epstein would tire of her. Helen's daughter, Kathy, married the poet and writer Laurie Lee.

---

7   Guggenheim, Peggy, *Out of This Century* (Deutsch 2005).

Ruth had several children by different men. Lorna married Ernest Wishart and had a son, the painter Michael Wishart, and, later, had an illegitimate daughter with Laurie Lee and, later still, had an affair with the painter Lucian Freud, modelling for many of his paintings. Freud, in turn, had a child with Kitty Garman Epstein.

My apologies for any mistakes and to anyone else whose offspring may feel left out (and may have visited Yew Tree Cottage).

# DANIEL MARC COHN-BENDIT

## French-German student revolutionary leader

**July 1968. Bastille Day. 10 pm. Paris. The beginning of the end of a long summer of revolt.**

Above all else, the wail upon wail of sirens. Ambulances. Police cars. Fire trucks. Smoke from burning tyres piled in front of barricades built of office furniture. Shouts of protest. Shouts of defiance. Barked orders. Broken glass crackling underfoot. The smell of hatred.

'*Tenez bon, camarades! A bas de Gaulle! Vive la liberté étudiante!*'

Flames shoot skyward from an exploding petrol tank of a yellow *deux chevaux*. People scatter as a captured police Citroën is driven into the wreckage. Three young people leap out, one firing a spray of red paint against a workshop wall.

*Danny Cohn-Bendit, 2018.* Heinrich-Böll-Stiftung.

He writes: '*Il est interdit d'interdine.*'

Everywhere, posters. Posters fresh, posters torn, posters defaced:

'*Mai 1968, debut d'une lutte prolongée.*' '*Sous les paves, la plage!*' '*L'imagination au pouvoir!*'

A crowbar is thrust into my hands, the wild youth pointing at the cobbles.

'*Creusez pour la victoire,*' he yells.

I do as I am bid. Molotov cocktails with their lighted tails fly overhead. The first stone set is hard to shift but, as it pops up, others follow easily. Beneath is yellow sand. Eager hands scoop up the ammunition and throw them with careful lobs to fall on the advancing riot shields.

'*Prenez ça, cochons fascistes.*' '*Je t'aime! Je le dis-le avec les pavés.*'

I am hit by a stray stone and fall. I stagger to a shop doorway full of rubble and discarded and unpleasant detritus.

Above me another poster:

'*Cela nous concerne tous.*'

Massed ranks of sweating *Compagnies Républicaines de Sécurité* (CSV) followed by enthusiastic Paris police sweep past. One kicks me to check that I am unconscious. Encumbered by long truncheons, they try to scale the walls of desks and chairs, lashing out at anything human wearing an armband. Socialist students, leftists and communists wear red; the anarchists choose black.

Tourists return from dinner after Bastille celebrations. They scream in fear and huddle together, but it is no protection.

From atop one pile, a red-haired protestor shouts insults and gives encouragement while waving a banner, perhaps an image of a stage play to come. I see him clearly.

'*C'est Dany le Rouge*,' shout idolisers. '*Vive Dany le Rouge.*'

There is a new miserable smell, that of fresh blood. All around, bodies with broken bones, deep cuts and forever bruises lie tangled. Amidst the carnage, there is a sudden if temporary silence. Dany (if it was him), the workers and the students have fled in order. The CSV in blood lust is in pursuit.

Near me, another spray painter continues the good work.

'3M' appears for '*Marx, Mao, Marcuse*'.

A man in factory overalls picks up a stray brick and heaves it at a shop window. I haul myself to my feet to escape the large shards of glass looking for a target. It is a furnishing shop.

'*Vite*,' I am instructed, '*trouver des couvertures pour les blessés.*'

I climb inside and re-emerge with a pile of gaudy summer beach towels. They are snatched from me and wrapped around the fallen.

An hour later, I walk down a side street a mile away, searching for my hotel. All is quiet. There is no sign of damage or discontent.

July 2014. Brussels. The European Parliament. The middle of the federalist project.

Daniel Cohn-Bendit, born 1945, is a French-German politician and leader of the Greens-European Free Alliance in the parliament. He was a student leader during the unrest of May 1968, known as *Dany le Rouge* for his politics and his hair.

Cohn-Bendit was born stateless to a German-Polish Ashkenazi Jewish family. (My mother took a DNA test and discovered that way back she was of significant Ashkenazi descent). Cohn-Bendit's parents were German Jews who fled the Nazis in 1933, his father a lawyer, Trotskyist and atheist. Daniel became German in 1959 and French in 2015.

In 2001, it was revealed, according to *Wikipedia*, that Cohn-Bendit had authored a 1976 article in the cultural-political magazine, *das da*, in which he graphically described engaging in sexual activities with children under his care at a Frankfurt kindergarten. In 2013, a recording was discovered wherein Cohn-Bendit discussed an 'incredibly erotic game' with a minor. Cohn-Bendit claimed the described activities were not based on true events and were an 'obnoxious provocation'.

# JOHN JULIUS COOPER, 2ND VISCOUNT NORWICH
English historian, travel book writer and TV performer

# 'FORGOTTEN'
## Celebrated British actress

*John Julius Norwich.* BBC.   *A small hand slid ...* freep!k.

It is fate. One never knows who is going to occupy the seat next to you on an airplane, or, on a really unlucky day, either side of you.

There was a time when I seemed to be on a plane every fortnight, most often travelling up and down from Edinburgh to London. It used to be called *The Shuttle*. No seats in advance; the next flight supposedly loading as soon as the one before took off. You were guaranteed a flight as long as you turned up in set time limits. It never worked well for me although I did get offered a top London hotel room, which I didn't want, because I met the criteria, but was the only one left and ready for the next flight. The alternative was just me on the plane.

I hated those cramped seats in the early morning, the feeling of rush and squeeze, the arbitrary and tasteless food, the overhead racks stuffed with briefcases and damp overcoats, the crying babies, the on-the-edge stewardesses.

One morning, escaping from the Edinburgh snow, I heaved a deep sigh of resentment and slid into a central seat of three. It was all that was on offer, all other inner and outer seats seem to be gone without exploring the back of the aircraft. I might have taken the free seat next to the aisle, but knew from experience that this would cause consternation and nasty looks later on. I always kept an ear open in case I had been in training with one of the pilots. It might mean an invite up to the cockpit away from the stress and the smells. Fat chance.

I had instinctively chosen this particular row because squashed against the window was a young lady, perhaps twenty-five years. This was no closet voyeurism, but a recognition that slim female rather than fat man equals more space.

I settled in, gave up on the newspaper because I had forgotten to buy one and all free copies had already gone, when a small hand, hot and dry, slid over the armrest. Perhaps because it did not meet any rejection from me, the hand tightened considerably on mine like a limpet. I looked, but the woman was facing straight ahead with her eyes squeezed shut.

I recognised the situation. This was a serious 'Fear of Flying' moment.

I muttered something like, 'Don't worry. It'll be OK.'

There was no response and that was how we lasted for an hour. I drank some coffee one handed. She didn't flinch or react to the cursory offer from the stewardess or to the smell of the drink.

The stewardess saw the locked hands, knew what was happening, grimaced and busied on.

We landed at Heathrow, but I was still firmly clutched. As the plane doors opened, she finally released me. The marks from her fingernails stayed deep and white in my skin for many more minutes.

'Thank you,' was all she said, eyes still shut.

Next day, as I flicked through the newspaper in my hotel room, I saw a photograph of a glamourous British actress, down from Edinburgh to open her new film at Leicester Square. She was the sort of person any red-blooded male would be happy to sit close to for an hour.

Of course, it was her, but I had not recognised her. And, now, perhaps fifty years on, I have made it worse because I have completely forgotten her name.

Several years later, on a flight to Paris, I sat next to a gentleman I thought I did recognise. I approached him delicately in case the last thing he wanted to do was to talk to stranger. He was one of my literary heroes, the historian John Julius Norwich. In fact, to prove the point, I showed him my current book, one of his, luckily new and in hardback with my page marker half way through.[8]

To break the ice, I told him my story of the young actress. He laughed heartily and I warmed to the man. We got talking and I told him about my current private research into the felt-hat industry around Bristol. To my surprise, he was most interested and plied me with questions for half an hour.

'As you know,' he said, 'I've done a lot of radio and TV work and sometimes I think that's all people know me from. It's so nice just to talk about history with someone who knows their subject.'

I beamed, lapping up the compliment.

Norwich, in fact Viscount Norwich, was the host of the BBC radio panel game, *My Word!*, for four years and also a regional contestant on *Round Britain Quiz*. He eventually presented some thirty TV documentaries covering Constantinople, Napolean, Cortés and Montezuma, Turkish antiquaries, Maximilion of Mexico. Toussaint of Haiti, the Knights of Malta and so forth. He knew fellow traveller Alun Chalfont well.

But, it was his written work that appealed most to me, especially as an expert on the Mediterranean civilisations. Several of his books have lasted the culling of my shelves.

Norwich was the son of Conservative politician and diplomat Duff Cooper and Lady Diana Manners, a celebrated beauty and society figure. Through his father, he was descended from King Willian IV and his mistress Dorothea Jordan. After a degree in French and Russian at New College, Oxford, Norwich joined the British Foreign Service and served in Yugoslavia and Lebanon. He took over his father's title, but lost the right with the House of Lords Act in 1999.

Norwich married twice, secondly to the Hon. Mary Phillips, daughter of The 1st Baron Sherfield. He was also the father of Allegra Huston, born of his affair

---

8  Norwich, John Julius, *Byzantium, The Decline and Fall* (Knopf 1996).

with the American ballet dancer Enrica Soma while she was married to the American film director John Huston.

I was sad when the plane landed. This was a man I could have talked to for many hours. The breadth of his knowledge was immense and he parted with it easily and without pretension. He did invite me to lunch at the House of Lords, but you know how it goes.

# THOMAS FREDERICK COOPER

## Welsh comedian

Tommy Cooper was pre-eminent among the handful of comedians who were at the height of their careers during the hey-days of commercial television. His large frame, trademark red fez, and a stage littered with failed magic tricks, made him one of the nation's favourites. It was enough for him to place his outstretched hands over a top hat, muttering, 'Just like that', with the rabbit failing to appear, for live audiences to convulse in laughter.

*Tommy Cooper.*

It was Cooper's death, aged sixty-three, that finally set him apart. In 1984, a London Weekend Television variety show was broadcast live from Her Majesty's Theatre in central London. Midway through his act, Cooper collapsed from a heart attack in front of twelve million viewers.

An assistant helped Cooper put on a golden cloak for a sketch. Jimmy Tarbuck, the host comedian, hidden behind the stage curtains, waited to secretly pass him props. Cooper slumped into a sitting position and the assistant smiled at him believing it was part of the act. The audience laughed, but Cooper fell back dying. The TV screen went black before an unscheduled commercial break. Cooper was pulled through the curtains. The show continued with the singer Howard Keel performing while the curtains twitched behind him as efforts were made to revive Cooper. It was his second heart attack on stage; the last in 1977 in Rome. Cooper was dead by the time the ambulance reached Westminster Hospital. Ghouls can watched the collapse today on YouTube.

Two aspects of Tommy Cooper's character contributed to my 'personal moment' with him.

His biographer, John Fisher, wrote, 'Everyone agrees that Cooper was mean (despite leaving a third of a million pounds at his death). Quite simply, he was acknowledged as the tightest man in show business, with a pathological dread of reaching into his pocket.' One of Cooper's stunts was to pay the exact taxi fare and, when leaving the cab, slip something into the driver's pocket, saying, 'Have a drink on me.' That something was a tea bag.

Cooper was also an alcoholic and his professionalism and reputation were seriously impaired in his later years. He also suffered from chronic indigestion, lumbago, sciatica, bronchitis and had severe circulation problems in his legs. He cut down on his drinking as a result, but never kicked the habit. On the Michael Parkinson show, he forgot to set the safety catch on a guillotine illusion. Only a last-minute intervention by the floor manager saved Parkinson from serious injury or worse.

From 1955, for almost thirty years until his death, Tommy Cooper lived with his family at 51, Barrowgate Road in Chiswick. His son, Thomas, born in 1956, was christened locally at Christ Church in Turnham Green, when the guests included Norman Wisdom and Harry Seacombe. The detached Edwardian house proved convenient for Cooper's TV work which was often filmed at Teddington. Regular house guests included Roy Hudd, Eric Sykes and Jimmy Tarbuck. The building was also stuffed with Cooper's props and magic gadgets. His ashes were scattered in the back garden over his favourite daffodils. There is a blue plaque on display on the front wall.

I worked in Chiswick in the 1970s. The nearest quiet pub for a pint before driving home was the *Queen's Head* in Sutton Lane only a minute or two's walk from Cooper's home. It is still there.

In the middle of a hushed discussion about the day's events, the door would crash back against the wall and a couple of outstretched hands appear. A lengthy giggle ensued, followed by, 'Just like that'. Then Tommy Cooper walked in, usually already the worse for drink. He would chose an occupied table at random and try a line like, 'Are you going to let me buy my own drink. If you don't cough up, I'll turn you into a rabbit … if I can remember how to do it.'

At the bar, the drink was already poured. The luckless victim usually quickly coughed up. I was caught three times, from memory. What was funny the first time, became a bore. I never knew Cooper buy his own drink and certainly not for anyone else. To his credit, he never tried the same people a second time on the same evening.

# ÉDITH JEANNE THÉRÈSE CRESSON

## French Prime Minister

Only a newspaper photograph at the head of page three reminded me of my briefest of contacts with Édith Cresson, shortly to become the first women Prime Minister of France. The photograph in *France-Soir* showed Madame Cresson reaching upwards through a crowd to shake my hand.

The paper was infamous for printing false information and promulgating wild conspiracy theories. In this case, the headline above the photograph suggested that Cresson, a leading socialist and career politician, already knew me. They asked in large type, 'Did she have a previous relationship with this unknown man?' The clasping of hands was too intimate, they suggested, for a casual first meeting.

*Édith Cresson, 1997.* Christian Lambiotte, European Communities.

*France-Soir* was in a downward spiral. Desperate action was needed to reinvigorate sales. The paper was on Cresson's case as rumours of indiscretions and malpractice swirled around her previous appointments as a member of the European parliament.

The truth was that at the time that the picture was taken, early in 1991, nor at any other time, did I know her. I was a tourist casually shopping in a mall in *La Défense*, a purpose built business district to the west of Paris, abounding in modern architecture and with over 200 stores. I saw a clutch of excited people and moved to its edge. In its midst stood Cresson with some minders and a couple of photographers. She was on the campaign trail looking for easy Press coverage.

For some reason, she caught my eye and held it as she moved several metres in my direction, reached through the other gogglers, and our hands touched. Her fingers were warm and, as she squeezed gently, I felt a small tremor of sexual excitement.

Then she was gone.

I did not see the photograph until a month or two later when a friend who had cut it out and saved it showed it to me. At first, I struggled to remember the occasion. No one else mentioned it at the time or since.

The hint of a scandal died at birth.

Later that year, Cresson was appointed prime minister in President Francois Mitterrand's government. She had held several ministerial appointments in the previous ten years: agriculture, foreign trade and tourism, industrial development and foreign trade and European affairs. Her tenure as prime minister was one of the shortest in the history of the Fifth Republic. She was quickly unpopular with the electorate and left office in less than twelve months. She strongly criticised Japanese trade practices and compared the Japanese with 'yellow ants trying to take over the world' which led to charges of racism. She also opined, 'Homosexuality seems strange to me. It's different and marginal. It exists more in the Anglo-Saxon tradition than the Latin one.'

Notwithstanding Cresson's briefest affair with me, it was real scandal that brought her down and ended her career.

She began her political offices as mayor of Thuré, a commune in the Vienne department in the Nouvelle-Aquitaine region in western France in 1977 and, in 1983, of the larger regional centre, Châtellerault, not far away. She became a member of the National Assembly for Vienne and a member of the European Parliament for France. After her prime ministership, she was appointed European Commissioner for Research, Science and Technology.

It was during this commissionership that her past caught up with her. She was the principal target in the fraud allegations that led to the resignation of the Santer Commission in 1999. The Commission members, who oversaw the introduction of the Euro, were all forced to resign over allegations of corruption. After the fraud enquiry, the European Commission said that Cresson had 'failed to act in response to known, serious and continuing irregularities over several years'.

Cresson was found guilty of not reporting failures in a youth training programme from which vast sums of money went missing.

In 2006, the European Court of Justice declared that Cresson breached her obligations as a Commissioner. The breach called for the imposition of a penalty, but the Court held that the finding of a breach was sufficient punishment and decided not to deprive her of her right to a pension and other benefits.

Brussels always finds a way to look after its own.

# PETE CREW

## English rock climber

Most of my difficulties at school stemmed from my rock climbing for which weekends in North Wales, specifically the Llanberis Pass, were essential.[9] It was something over a hundred miles and took four hours of determined hitchhiking when I couldn't organise a lift. In those days, hitchhiking was a friendly and expected way of travel for the young. A rucksack with a prominent dirty-white nylon climbing rope often eased the way.

I was seldom left standing for more than an hour. Many drivers expected an intelligent conversation and the subjects covered, and the education and shared experience received, were part and parcel of growing up.

*Pete Crew on Great Wall, Clogwyn Du'r Arddu.*

To reach the rock cliffs as the afternoon darkened, it was better to leave school at mid-day so I wore as much of my climbing clothes as was permitted on Friday mornings. I collected my gear from the maths study at the lunch break and headed west. Only one lesson was missed – maths again – and that could be sorted out with my teacher at the local *Coach and Horses*.

The trouble was the return trip because two full days' climbing meant striking tent early on Monday. Lifts were seldom easy in the hills at first light, often short hops shared in the back of aged, spring-damaged Landrovers with a

---

9  Heal, Chris, *Disappearing*, Chapter 1 (C&S 2023, 2nd edition).

couple of panting Collie sheepdogs. Some days I was lucky and back in lessons by mid-morning.

I soon found that to clump in half-way through a discussion on Molière was seen as disruptive and disrespectful. I learned to make my entrance between lessons, but matters started to get out of hand as my classmates began to bet on my arrival time. The week's result were posted on a school noticeboard with the winner identified and their share of the pot. I tried hard to work my way through this, but the best way, I found, was to drop French as a subject so as to curtail the embarrassment.

In retaliation, the school declined to enter me for the French public examination, but a sympathetic and loan-heavy teacher did that for me, even paying the registration fee against a written-off personal debt. The last morning lesson was maths and I was regularly given a firm, loud and public dressing down and told to, 'See me afterwards'. However, this recent graduate was also a devoted climber and 'afterwards' meant our disciplinary talks were held in the Coach and Horses where he quizzed me in great detail on my latest ascents.

When in Llanberis Pass, I camped because from a tent it was simple to get to the foot of the crags. These routes, with the standards rising each year, were and still are considered severe and classic across the UK and round the world. I went back many years later and was struck by the difference. The road had turned into a car park with small parties waiting patently in line for their allotted time to take on a beginner's slot. I had been there in the wild days: wild places and even wilder people.

My skills and strength were limited by my above-average height. The legend of the fifties, Joe Brown, was the man to follow and soon became the man to beat. Pete Crew and Martin Boysen led the challengers. If Brown broke in a new climb, Crew repeated it and faster. Brown was not above covering handholds with a sod of earth to slow down or put off usurpers.

In 1962, a strong climber called Dave Sales fell off *Quietus*, a Brown climb, both runners ripped free and he died. At a mountaineering school, I later knew another of the aspirants, David 'Rowdy' Yates, who walked with a pronounced limp from one day trying too hard. He was philosophical, but it obviously still hurt.

The first assaults of *Great Wall* and *The Boldest* on Clogwyn Du'r Arddu marked the apex of Crew's climbing career.[10] Both routes utilised what some regraded as cheating tactics with several points of aid and a bolt. *Cloggy* is a north-facing rhyolite set of cliffs located on the northern flank of Snowdon. It is considered to be one of the best traditional climbing areas in Britain, 'the shrine of British climbing', and a 'crucible for the development of most of the finest climbers in Britain and the scene of many of their finest achievements'.

I watched Crew many times, standing below with his flop of dirty fair hair, a stump of cigarette balanced on a lower lip and dark glasses, assessing the route. I have never seen anyone climb so quickly while on the edge and in whatever the weather. He had a clear eye for the shortest, most direct route. He made liberal use of nuts and bolts jammed into crevices to protect himself against falls. He redefined 'impossible'. It was Crew who introduced me to the intricacies of hand-jamming, which he said he had picked up from Brown. Anyone can jam a hand into a small crack and flex it so that the fist provides a painful wedge to hang from. It's the wide ones, he said, that took the skill.

'Look at the crack once, shove your arm in and look away. Feel until it is right, then, just pull up to the next move. Never look into it, you'll keep fiddling about until your strength ebbs away.'

That lesson led to my one climb with him. He had arrived early at a new pitch to be named *Yellow Wall* from the tiny flowers in the ledges and found he was without a partner. The weather was set for heavy rain. He knew I could hold him if needed – I was needed twice. The climb took him just over the hour as he ferreted his way, but it took me twice the time and I had his route and shouted instructions to follow.

---

10 Ward, Mick, *The Vector Generation*, 21/5/2020.

# NGUYEN SINH CUNG

## Hồ Chí Minh, founder and first President of the Democratic Republic of Vietnam

Hồ Chí Minh was born Nguyễn Sinh Cung probably in 1890 and died in 1969. He was colloquially known as 'Uncle Ho' (*Bác Hồ*) and was the founder and first President of the Democratic Republic of Vietnam. These details are important because I met him and spent personal time with him in 2015 when he had been dead for over forty years.

*Hồ Chí Minh, c. 1946.*

I arrived at Ho's mausoleum very early on a dark Tuesday morning in pouring rain. It is a large, grey granite monumental building, inspired by Lenin's tomb in Moscow. The whole is more than twenty metres high and over forty metres wide. It is sited in the centre of the immense parade square of Ba Dinh in Hanoi. The square is where Ho read his country's Declaration of Independence in 1945 which established the Vietnamese Democratic Republic. I read in my guide book that the surrounding gardens have nearly 250 different species of plants and flowers from across Vietnam, although, in the downpour and from under my umbrella, there was little to admire apart from scale. A sodden Vietnamese flag hung limply from a dominating white flagpole.

Between two out-of-season frangipani trees, two soldiers, very smart but already soaked, rigidly guarded the entrance with automatic weapons. There were no other visitors in sight which surprised me as I had been told at my hotel that over 15,000 people paid their respects each week. I stood at the bottom of the steps waiting for something to happen. Nothing did. I wondered if I had chosen a day when the mausoleum was closed.

An officer complete with two semi-automatic side pistols in white hip holsters appeared in the portico and summoned me with a snap of fingers. I climbed the steps checking that I had my passport with me. This captain had a jet black pencil moustache on his top lip which managed to hide any semblance of smile lines. His eyes were small, black and without emotion. I have been among soldiers of foreign countries many times, however, sometimes, like that day, sensible nervousness brings an outward show of deference.

'Chào buổi sáng,' *Good morning, Sir*, I offered.

The fingers snapped again, twice. This meant, 'Show me your papers, immediately'. My passport was taken inside while I waited in the wet. There was no break in the low cloud which all but merged with the building's roof. The soldiers were impervious and unblinking.

A few minutes later, the officer returned and handed me back my passport.

'There is no need for you to try to speak Vietnamese,' he said. 'I speak English perfectly well. Why were you standing at the bottom of the steps in the rain?'

'I was waiting for President Ho Chi Minh's mausoleum to open,' I explained. 'I came early because I did not want to be swept along with the crowds and given little time to pay my respects. But it seems like it is closed?'

'Why do you think that it is closed?'

'Because there are no visitors here.'

'Well, you are wrong. It is open. But you are right, there are no visitors. It seems like the early hour and the heavy rain have put people off. I can only wish that the Vietnamese people would show as much respect as you, a foreigner, have done to our great hero and international communist. You are most welcome. Please come in and, as you are alone, you may take your time. You have a rare opportunity for deep and personal reflection.'

He turned unexpectedly to face me directly.

'Did you know that around this mausoleum seventy-nine cycad trees have been planted, one for each year of the president's life?'

I did know that cycads were stout, slow-growing, long-life trees of many varieties that have naked seed pods, but I thought it best to show gratitude for the information so freely given. I bowed and made a traditional gesture of thanks.

I shared that the day before I had met with Mr Huu Ngoc at his Hanoi home for a long chat over tea. Mr Huu was a former friend and translator to Ho Chi Minh. He wrote then for the newspapers *Le Courier Vietnam* and the *Vietnam News*.

'Perhaps you are more than just a tourist,' said my officer.

The front hall is clad with pink-veined marble bearing the inscription 'Nothing is more precious than Independence and Freedom' over Uncle Ho's signature inlaid in gold. Ho's marble-lined chamber is in the centre of the mausoleum. The embalmed body lies on a metal bed on a stone pedestal in a glass case. He wears his old khaki peasant uniform with a pair of rubber sandals at his feet. The morticians have done their work well. He looks at peace.

There are two rows for visitors to file past, the inner row reserved for children. No speaking, no photography, nor food or drink is allowed. Soldiers stood stiff at each corner of the case otherwise the room was empty. An order had clearly already been given and I was nodded into the inner children's row and, instead of being rushed through in a great flow of traffic, allowed to stand, head bent, in front of the great man. This is why I feel I can claim this meeting as a true personal moment and eligible for this book.

For a large part of the Vietnam war, I lived near Edinburgh. I swapped *The Scotsman* for *The Times* as I believed their coverage of the conflict and its causes to be far better. I was never confident with the war. Certainly when I thought of its architects, Dwight Eisenhower, John Kennedy, Richard Nixon, Lyndon Johnson and Gerald Ford, then Uncle Ho, let down so badly by the French and Americans, and who now lay before me, towered above them all in intellect and character.

Here was the founder of the French Communist Party in Paris in 1920, a student in Moscow, founder of the Vietnamese Revolutionary Youth League in 1925, leader of the Việt Minh against the Japanese during the second world war and, in 1945, leader of the fight against the monarchy and proclaimer of a republic. When the French returned to power in order to claim the rubber for their motor tyre industry, he retreated to the countryside and initiated guerilla warfare. He defeated the French at the Battle of Điện Biên Phủ. He then led the north of the artificially divided country and fought the corrupt American-supported south, overseeing the transport of troops and supplies along the Ho Chi Minh trail until his death in 1969.

The day's first visitors entered a little sheepishly and interrupted my reminiscences. As I reached the steps, my erstwhile inquisitor appeared. He waved and he smiled. I did the same.

The sun had come out. It was humid and warm. Steam was rising from the multi-coloured pathways. I made my way through the long lawn into Bac Son Street, lined with red roses and peach blossoms. At the street's end was the Martyrs' Memorial where I stood quietly paying my respects before moving on to the Ho Chi Minh Museum and, next door, Uncle's final home, a simple, unadorned and sparsely furnished stilt house.

# REGINALD KENNETH DWIGHT

## Sir Elton Hercules John, British singer and songwriter

Surely no one needs me to explain who Elton John is?

Well, OK, a bit.

Reginald Dwight is one of the best-selling music artists of all time with over 300 million records worldwide. He had, to date, more than fifty top-40 hits on the UK Singles Chart and US Billboard Hot 100 as well as seven consecutive 'number one' albums. He is the most successful solo artist in the history of Billboard; his tribute single to Diana, Princess of Wales, *Candle in the Wind 1997*, a rewritten version of his 1974 single, sold over thirty-three million copies worldwide and is the best-selling chart single of all time.

*Elton John, 2024. Raph_PH.*

Dwight changed his name in 1972 using the names of two fellow band members in the Bluesology jazz band: Elton Dean and Long John Baldry. His middle name of Hercules came from the name of the horse in the British sitcom *Steptoe and Son*, of which Dwight was a big fan.

John's songwriting partnership with lyricist Bernie Taupin is one of the most successful in history. He has also composed music for musical films and theatre: *The Lion King* (1994), *Aida* (2000) and *Billy Elliot, the Musical* (2005).

He is an HIV/AIDS charity fundraiser bringing in £300 million since 1992. He was chairman of Watford Football Club. In the late 1970s to the late

1980s, John developed a severe drug and alcohol addiction, but claims he has been sober since 1990. In 2014, he married his long-term partner, Canadian filmmaker David Furnish.

So, that's the Elton John I'm talking about.

The 2019 *Sunday Times Rich List* gave John an estimated fortune of £320 million. In 2000, he admitted spending £30 million in just under two years – and average of £1.5 million a month on property, flowers and cars. In 2001, John sold twenty of his cars at Christie's auction house for nearly £2 million saying that as he was out of the country so often he never had a chance to drive them. The sale included a 1993 Jaguar XJ220 at £234,750, and several Ferraris, Rolls-Royces and Bentleys.

It was because of these cars, or rather one of the Rollers, that I met the great man, if only fleetingly. I was driving a yellow Ford Cortina estate in the West End of London. This big black car loomed up beside me and we touched. There was a bit of a scrape above its front wheel arch but, when I got out to check, no dent. My car was a collection of scratches so I couldn't be sure of any new damage.

The chauffeur walked around looking for a fight.

'Don't bully me,' I said. 'Your Rolls doesn't give you ownership of the road. You shouldn't have tried to cut in.' I had been drinking. He started to square up.

The back door window slid noiselessly down and this chap half leaned out.

It was him. I mean him, you know.

He seemed a bit languid, more bored than upset.

'I don't want to be late,' he said to the gathering audience as if it was all their fault. 'Can we get going?'

I don't think that he noticed me. He certainly glided away without even giving me his address.

When I read several years later that Sir Elton had made good money by appearing in a series of commercials for *Diet Coke*, the *Royal Mail*, *Snickers* and *John Lewis* department stores, I stopped worrying about the cost to him of having his paintwork redone. It had been getting to me.

So, if you bought one of the man's cars in the Christie sale and you noticed a dodgy bit of paintwork above a nearside front wheel, now you know what happened.

# SIR STEPHEN JOHN FRY

## English actor, comedian and presenter

Stephen Fry and I met in the downstairs toilet at *The Ivy* restaurant in West Street opposite London's Ambassadors and St Martin's theatres. Or, to be completely accurate, and to safeguard our reputations, at the door to the gentlemen's toilet.

What can one say about Fry's artistic career that is any more than a list of achievements (although I have to say that his style is not always my cup of tea. So often, it seems, he overplays and replays the same part). One worries about criticism given his much recorded mental health problems, particularly when acting has proved too much for him. Since 2011, Fry has been president of the charity *Mind* and was knighted this year, 2025, for his services to mental health awareness.

*Stephen Fry, 2024.* Elena Ternovaja.

OK. I accept. I have to list some of Fry's achievements.

He has received eleven BAFTA Award nominations for his work in television, so what do I know. For his performance as Oscar Wilde in *Wilde* (1998), he earned a nomination for the Golden Globe Award for Best Actor in motion picture drama. He won the Screen Actors Guild Award for Outstanding Performance along with the ensemble of the Robert Altman directed murder mystery *Gosford Park* (2001). On Broadway, he received two Tony Award nominations for Best Book of a Musical for *Me and My Girl* (1987) and Best Featured Actor in a Play for his performance as Malvolio in the revival of William Shakespeare's *Twelfth Night* (2014).

None of which counts his honorary Doctor of Laws from Dundee University (1995) and another honorary Doctorate, this time in Letters from the University of East Anglia (1999) and there are many others at home and abroad. He was the last person to be named Pipe Smoker of the Year (2003) before the award was discontinued.

Fry, born in 1957, has claimed relationship with the Fry chocolate family; John Fry, one of the signatories to the death warrant of Charles I; and with the cricketer C B Fry. All of these notwithstanding that his mother is Jewish and his maternal grandparents were Hungarian. Other ancestors were deported from Vienna to a Nazi ghetto in Riga where they perished. His mother's aunt and cousins were sent to Auschwitz and Stutthof and never seen again.

Fry married Elliott Spencer in 2015.

*The Ivy*, when I met Fry was in its glorious later period before its temporary closure due to a change in ownership in 1989. It reopened the following year with a transformational design and one hundred seats plus a sixty-seat private dining space upstairs. Mobile phones and cameras are forbidden and there is a smart casual dress code. The modern *Ivy* has since expanded across the United Kingdom and Ireland with its new restaurants known as the *Ivy Collection*.

The London restaurant with its excellent food is, naturally, because of its location, popular with theatregoers. It became a theatrical institution with *habitués* like Laurence Olivier, Vivian Leigh, Marlene Dietrich, John Gielgud, Lilian Braithwaite, Terence Rattigan, Binkie Beaumont and Noël Coward.

It was a long-held ambition fulfilled when I finally sat down at a central table. Along the external walls, in the posh seats, a dozen stars were ensconced at their regular spots, too many to mention and none of whom I met (and tried not to stare at too hard as I tried to remember their names).

The lamb cutlets melted in the mouth and the creamed spinach was a revelation. This way of cooking this vegetable is now a staple in our household.

The toilets at *The Ivy* also set a gold standard: stiff cotton serviettes and dozens of bottles of soaps, perfumes and sprays. Stephen Fry and I arrived at the door at the same time, me coming out and him going in. We both stepped back, waved the other forward through the open door and uttered an obligatory, 'Sorry'.

Fry smiled widely.

'You realise,' he said, 'that we have just had an English moment.'

# ERICH ERNST HEINRICH GERTH AND GEORG CARL GERTH

## WWI Kapitänleutnants, u-boat commanders and brothers

*Erich and Georg Gerth. Cover of* Sound of Hunger.

Technically, well actually, this pair of WWI u-boat commanders don't meet the criteria for inclusion in this book. There was no way that I could have met them. Erich, the elder brother, was killed by the Gestapo in 1943 while riding in a taxi to the airport in Rome with his son Marco in the front seat. Two men Marco had never seen before, he told me, and never saw again, sat either side of Erich. He did not speak, went red in the face, and died quickly. Georg survived two world wars and died in 1970. For the last three years, he was mute, slept on a mattress on the floor kept in by side supports. He suffered from dementia, was helpless and needed intimate care.

The reason that I have included these two men is that I probably knew them better than almost every other person in this book for I researched and wrote about them copiously, including their biographies, and know their living families in the United States and in Bavaria.[11]

---

11 Heal, Chris, *Saints & Sinners, The career of Kapitänleutnant Erich Gerth 1886-1943,* and *The War of the Raven, The career of Kapitänleutnant Georg Gerth 1888-1970* (both C&S, 2023).

Altogether in three books that together amounted to over 1,300 pages, I believe they have earned their place.

I found the brothers by chance. I finished my history doctorate at Bristol University when I was sixty-five years old. I cleared the many sub-projects and obligations and had some free time. Early in 2016, I contacted the Marine Archaeology Trust in Southampton as a potential volunteer. The Trust had developed a five-year Heritage Lottery venture as part of the centenary jamboree commemorating World War I. Called *Forgotten Wrecks*, the intention was to chart and record some seven hundred south coast sites that resulted from the conflict, some on land and many uncelebrated or even unknown.

To begin, I was given two shipwrecks to investigate, the *Minerva* and the *Broomhill*, both merchant steamers, and, as was quickly obvious, sunk a few miles apart on the same day in 1917 and, therefore, most likely, by u-boat. The culprit was *UC-61*, a coastal mine-layer, which, after detaching her mines, had forced with gunfire 'my' two boats to stop, encouraged their crews into lifeboats, and then boarded and set bombs on their waterlines. Research at The National Archives in Kew, London, established seven other vessels attacked by the same u-boat on the south coast and which I attached to the *Forgotten Wrecks* project.

There followed a hunt for the *UC-61*. She was easy to find on the internet; in a small way the submarine had become a celebrity. The renown was not because of any heroic deeds, but because she had run aground in fog on the beach at Wissant a few miles south of Calais near *Cap Gris Nez*. Supposedly, *UC-61* and her captain, Georg Gerth, was the only u-boat to be captured by the Belgian cavalry. And her carcass still rests there on the sands, regularly visible at low tide.

The chase developed into an international hunt as I pursued *UC-61*'s career from her building yard at Bremen to the ignominy of the beach. I found records of Georg Gerth's crew with the Red Cross in Switzerland and in Berlin and tracked them as best I could through to their freedom or deaths. Gerth's story was the most remarkable. He was imprisoned on a French island on the Atlantic coast. Corresponding in secret ink with his home base in Belgium, he arranged for a u-boat to come from Bruges to try to rescue him. The attempt failed, but it is an exciting tale.

I soon took serious notice of Georg's elder brother, Erich. Erich joined the *Kaiserliche Marine* two years before Georg, but followed him into u-boat command two years later in 1918 and fought briefly in the Mediterranean alongside many famous names of the war. Erich's wider life was fascinating: spying with Wilhelm Canaris, later head of the *Abwehr*, the German military intelligence, in South America; connections to the Battle of Verdun and Baron von Richthofen, the fighter ace; marrying a Jewish countess; the Spartakist revolution and the murder of communist leaders Karl Liebknecht and Rosa Luxembourg; contact with a pope-to-be, Eugene Pacelli; covertly preparing a second u-boat fleet for the next war; attempts to stop World War 2 and involvement in the Nazi studios producing films like *The Blue Angel* with Marlene Dietrich.

It was a story that kept on giving.

The brothers' story was first published as *Sound of Hunger*.[12] It was an unusual and lengthy book, seeking to view the war from the bottom up rather than the more usual viewpoint of kings and queens. I wanted to understand how Erich and George, from a lowly middle class Prussian background, had joined the preening and exclusive German navy. A central argument of the book was that the British had deliberately engineered a food blockade and had starved to death almost a million German people, mostly women and children. This was an inconvenient and proven fact and provided ample justification for the u-boat response. It was truly a war of attrition. The different ways the Gerth brothers responded to their tasks shaped the rest of their lives.

In 2017, a hundred years from the wrecking of *UC-61*, I invited some twenty historians, local dignitaries, divers and enthusiasts, to join me at a day-long event at Wissant. Attendees came from France, Belgium, Germany and the UK. Pride of place went to Frau Christa-Maria Gerth, the last surviving child of Georg, and her two sons.

After visiting key sites, that evening, the Art and History Society of Wissant hosted a conference for two hundred people at which I talked about the life and last days of *UC-61* and her crew. In 2023, the society published a book in French, based on *Sound of Hunger*, for sale to the town's residents and many summer visitors which explained the piece of twisted metal on their beach.[13]

---

12 Heal, Chris, *Sound of Hunger* (Unicorn, 2018).
13 Heal, Chris et Lesoin, Henri, *La dernière patrouille de l'UC 61, Wissant 1917* (Art et Histoire de Wissant 2023).

# QADDURA MOHAMMED ABD AL-HAMID

## Moroccan terrorist and hotel bomber

*Security personnel assess the damage after the bomb attack at the Norfolk Hotel, 1980. My escape drainpipe is centre background.*

I'm sure that I saw Qaddura Mohammed Abd Al-Hamid at midday on New Year's Eve in 1980. I had just arrived at the Norfolk Hotel in Nairobi with my family. As we passed into reception, a man of clear Mediterranean complexion, medium height, dark brushed back hair, smart casual clothes, passed close by me toting a small, but full, overnight shoulder bag. He was moving firmly, not rushing, towards a waiting black taxi. The back door was opened for him and, as he bent to get in, I caught his eye directly. I felt, with what is today perhaps wishful hindsight, a chill.

My employer, an American multi-national, had offered me a job in Johannesburg for two years and my wife and I jumped at the chance to explore southern Africa, the extra money, an interesting job, the warmth, and to see apartheid at first hand and to form our own opinions, perhaps to help in small ways.

On our way out we flew first to Nairobi and travelled by car to Malindi for two weeks' beach holiday over Christmas.[14] The coast in those days was uncluttered, the resorts mostly a little worn, functioning but unsophisticated. The plan was always to return to Nairobi for New Year's Eve and then to fly to South Africa and our new life. I booked the iconic *Norfolk* in its leafy suburb. The hotel used to stand on the edge of the city, acting as the starting point for safaris for big game hunters like Theodore Roosevelt and Ernest Hemingway.

My wife took the children to the café near the entrance so that we could put them to bed early and enjoy the gala dinner and celebration. My son arrived breathlessly at my door to let me know they were settled for their meal and ran off. He ran everywhere. It was not long after eight o'clock.

I had just poured a gin and tonic and was in my dressing gown ready for a shower when the bomb went off. I found myself in a cloud of swirling dust, everything obscured, and that acrid never-to-be-forgotten mix of electrical charge and high explosives. The ceiling came down and I was trapped between the bed and heavy rafters which landed either side of my head. A fireball went through the room and took out the window to the courtyard from where I had just waved to my family. I wrenched my back badly getting out and stumbled to the door. The wide, carpeted stairs had gone. I went a bit numb and confused. I searched the room for my wallet, which I found, stuffed some clothes into one of the suitcases, climbed out onto the tiles and lowered myself down a drainpipe. Someone offered to store the case and I never saw it again. I walked in bare feet across the jagged blast damage to the hotel restaurant.

I found my family and we were bundled by panicked staff into the back of a commandeered van being driven across town to the hospital at breakneck pace, and it almost did as our heads were banged against the walls. I sat and watched the injured and dead being brought in, men without limbs, without skin, women without breasts, without clothes. After half an hour of chaos I had had enough and caught a lift, still in my bloodied gown, to the Hilton Hotel where my American Express card got me the last room.

I was woken by the chamber-maid at midday and remember little of the next week.

The bomb was planted by a Moroccan with a fake Maltese passport named Qaddura Mohammed Abd Al-Hamid, identified as a member of the Marxist

---

14 Heal, Chris, *Disappearing*, Chapter 6 (C&S 2023, 2nd edition).

Popular Front for the Liberation of Palestine (PFLP). Al-Hamid had a long history of plane hijacks and was involved in a machine-gun attack on passengers at Rome airport in 1973. Al-Hamid checked into the Norfolk as Muhammed Akila, quibbled about his noisy room, 203, and accepted number seven. For several days, he seldom went out, refused housekeeping, and was visited several times by an Arab woman who spoke with a pronounced German accent.

Al-Hamid placed his bomb under a radiator directly above the ballroom. Twenty people were killed and another eighty-seven wounded. The device would have killed many more except that it was sitting by mistake directly over a metal beam so that the blast went sideways.

The PFLP explained that the attack followed the successful storming of the airport buildings at Entebbe in Uganda four years before by Israeli commandos. An Air France airliner had been hijacked by the PFLP and over one hundred Jewish passengers held hostage. The bomb was in retaliation for the assistance given by the Kenyans to the Israelis who refuelled their aircraft in Nairobi on their way back home. The Norfolk was owned by the Jewish Block family so the choice of target was doubly appropriate.

Al-Hamid left the hotel about noon on the day of the bombing, room paid for in advance, and took a Kenya Airways flight to Jeddah in Saudi Arabia. He was in the air when the blast ripped through the restaurant.

And I had seen him.

The Kenyan Police kept people out of the hotel's wreckage for some time in fear of a second explosion. They used that time to strip the rooms of their valuables. All my cash, my wife's jewellery, suitcases, camera and the rest were gone. The hotel placed what was unstolen in sad heaps in an undamaged room and there the next day I found our four passports, a chess board bought as a memento, chess set gone, and two favourite furry toys, an elephant and a pig.

Before I was allowed to take my pathetic belongings away, I was asked to pay for the room. I refused and was threatened with arrest and was only let go after a large police sergeant forced me to sign a disclaimer against all loss.

Among the many losses was my son's favoured emu hand puppet. British Airways flew out a replacement, seated in the cockpit, two days' later.

I had an operation to remove a ruptured disc in my back and spent my first two months in Johannesburg in and out of hospital.

I can still see Al-Hamid's face today, but I have never seen a picture of him.

# CHESTER 'CHET' BAYARD HANSEN

## Aide to US General of the Army Omar Bradley, WWII

For most of his life, Chet Hansen worked as an aide to two of the great leaders of twentieth century America: General Omar Bradley and Thomas J Watson junior, son of the founder of the IBM Corporation and its long-term leader. I met Hansen over two days in the 1970s in Armonk, New York, IBM's headquarters with its neutered apple trees in the surrounding orchard. He introduced me to his staff. I was on a goodwill, fact finding trip from the UK.

Bradley picked Hansen early in the war when he was conducting training in Louisiana. Hansen was a journalism graduate from Syracuse University, drafted in 1941, and followed Bradley as he rose through the ranks. They were together during the North Africa campaign, the invasion of Sicily and as Bradley led US ground forces on D-day as commander of the First Army. Hansen twice landed under fire on the Omaha invasion beach to gather first-hand information for his boss and also cruised close along the shoreline for the same purpose.

*Chester Hansen.*

Hansen kept a diary ending at some 300,000 words whose details of war and military life have become a trove for historians. Now at the Army Heritage and Education Centre in Carlisle, Pennsylvania, they became a principal resource for many books, including Rick Atkinson's *An Army at Dawn* about the Allied invasion of North Africa, which won the Pulitzer Prize in 2003.

'He was a meticulous note-taker,' said Atkinson, 'and a keen observer. For someone trying to understand the nuances of the war and how personalities interacted or didn't interact, he is invaluable.'

Captain Chet Hansen appeared on screen working for Omar Bradley, played by the actor Stephen Young, in the epic American biographical supposedly 'warts and all' war film, *Patton*, starring George C Scott and Karl Malden as Bradley. Patton was one of Bradley's generals, wayward, but highly successful, who was often in contact with Hansen.

Hansen remained as an aide to Bradley after the war, promoted to colonel, following him – the last of the nation's five-star generals – as Bradley served in a series of high posts, including head of the Veterans Association in Washington, DC.[15] Hansen was effectively chief of public relations. Hansen also recorded hundreds of hours of conversation with the general and used them when he ghostwrote Bradley's best-selling war memoir reportedly getting half of all royalties.[16]

Chet Hansen spent time in the US Air Force and, then, the Central Intelligence Agency (CIA). He resigned his commission in 1956 and, after a couple of years in public relations, joined IBM as, initially, aide to its new CEO, Thomas J Watson junior, whose father had recently died.

Watson ran the IBM business with an iron hand, issuing rules, dress codes and cultural norms which reached into employees' homes, especially in the United States. The company was hugely successful with electric typewriters, punched card machines and the new-fangled computers, which were first thought to have a very limited market. Watson was soon spending nine per cent of turnover on research and development. To own early IBM stock meant becoming a rich investor with annual compound growth rates of around thirty per cent, much as the Apple and Microsoft businesses of recent times. *Fortune* called Watson 'the greatest capitalist in history' and *Time* listed him as one of the 'one hundred most influential people of the twentieth century'. Watson was national president of the Boy Scouts of America. On retirement, he was appointed by President Jimmy Carter as the US Ambassador to the Soviet Union from 1979 to 1981.

There seems no record of how Chet Hansen got on with Watson, although after so many years as an aide to Bradley, another powerful man although accounted a friend, pliability and delivery might have been core skills. For whatever reason, Hansen's journalistic background came to the fore and he

---

15 Kaufman, Leslie, 'Chester Hansen, 95, aide to top general detailed WWII history', *Boston News*, 27/10/2012.
16 Bradley, Omar N, *A Soldier's Story* (1951) – although credit for ghostwriting is given to A J Liebling.

became editor of the company's *Think* magazine. 'Think' was the company's slogan from Watson's father, and adorned almost every wall in the company.

When I visited Armonk, I was running the IBM UK company's shabby equivalent, a fortnightly newspaper without any great pretensions. *Think* was the opposite. Begun in 1935, it was, at first, a magazine that was only distributed externally, essentially for customers. In 1971, *Think* combined with IBM's employee magazine, *Business Machines*, and was only distributed internally. Its content was revered as a voice from on high.

Hansen held mythical power and was thought untouchable with his experience and contacts. The offices were lush and large with his own reputedly bigger than Watson's. The magazine's production values matched the best in the commercial market. Lavish sums, in my eyes, were spent on photography and artwork; few writers inside IBM made it to between the covers. Many of the contributors were commissioned and represented the nation's best talent in their areas of expertise. It is difficult to overemphasise the difference between my cramped meetings with a couple of staff members in London with the leisurely and respectful, but keenly fought, equivalents in Armonk.

All told, it was an extraordinary production that could only have been afforded, or permitted, at the richest and most self-regarding corporation in the world.

Hansen graciously introduced me to his key staff. I sat in on a few meetings. I found him a charming man, just in his sixties, with an easy manner, but underneath I suspected an iron fist in his velvet glove, not welcoming to indecision or flummery. The tiniest production details were inspected and inspected again. To be fair, the intent was always the highest quality, but at a fearsome price.

I think I received some referred awe from his employees as, if I ran the operation in London, I must have much of the power of a Hansen, the only comparison that they could make. If they only knew!

I was invited to have lunch on the second day having seemingly passed a test or two. About fifteen staff (I had two journalists and a borrowed administrator) drove with me to a local restaurant. This, I was told, was an unprecedented occasion during the working week. We had to return by two o'clock. Hansen did not attend, citing executive meetings.

'What would I like to drink?'

I hesitated for Armonk's no alcohol policy, stemming from Watson senior's day, was notorious.

'It's OK,' I was told quietly. 'Chet says he understands that the English like a beer with their lunch. He used to work in Europe during the war, you know. But we'll have to pay for it because it would never be allowed to go through expenses.' I thought of the pint-fuelled lunches we enjoyed in London.

I asked for a beer and stood the company a round. Two others joined me. For the rest, it was clearly a step too far and they stuck to water and juice. Being English, of course, I later had another one. I half expected there might be lightning flashes and heavy storms, but the kind sun continued as we drove back.

Over lunch, much of the conversation dwelled on how quickly one had to work on a fortnightly publication like mine with all the intrusive corporate approvals. Clearly, the pressure was thought excessive. 'How they would have fared on a daily?' I thought to myself.

One story about Chet did come out which I hope was true and not apocryphal which would have been disrespectful. It was certainly well attested. Apparently, Hansen kept a tank in his office, a present from old army comrades. It was pedal-powered, big enough for him to sit inside, and painted in the markings of one of Bradley's old armoured brigades. If Hansen got upset, he sometimes displayed his displeasure by driving in his tank down the corridors at Armonk looking for his adversary. When the culprit was cornered, Hansen's tank would fire cigars with some force as a punishment.

Hansen retired from IBM in 1986 and died in 2012 on his wife's birthday at the age of ninety-five. The couple share a grave at Arlington National Cemetery.

## SIR JACK ARNOLD HAYWARD

English businessman, philanthropist, owner of Wolverhampton Wanderers

## GRAEME MURRAY WALKER

English motorsport commentator

## SIR BERNARD INGHAM

Margaret Thatcher's chief Press secretary

*Statue of Jack Hayward, 2019, at the Molyneux, Wolverhampton.* Elliott Brown.

*Murray Walker, 2009.* Matthew Spencer, Flickr.

*Bernard Ingham.*

In May 1999, I sold my shares in my marketing consultancy and, after a series of personal contracts, decided that I wanted to do something completely different.

A long holiday was an obvious option and one possibility kept coming to my attention. It was a bit of an odd ball. A handful of former employees of the

Union-Castle Shipping Line, famous for its stately passenger liners and cargo ships between Europe and Africa from 1900 to 1977, yearned to recreate the old days. The idea was a 'centenary' voyage. It seems that as many of them were not, shall we say, in the top jobs, there was some wishful thinking. The cost of such a venture seemed out of touch.

These ex-employees did find a ship, an ageing, but still very serviceable, *MV Victoria*. Built on the Clyde in 1965 as the *MV Kungsholm*, she was originally a combined ocean liner and cruise ship. Rebuilt as a cruiser for P&O in 1978, she could carry over 400 passengers and a similar number of crew, although the enthusiasts didn't manage to sell all of the berths.

They also decided on a route – from Southampton around Africa and return over two months. Some of the ports of call were islands from my boyhood dreams, Madeira, Gran Canaria, St Helena and Ascension down the backbone of the Atlantic, several stops on the southern African coast, then Madagascar, Mauritius, Reunion, Seychelles, through the Suez Canal with calls for Petra and Jerusalem, and into the Mediterranean and home via Gibraltar.

What remained for the would-be adventurers was to find the money. I first saw the voyage advertised at nearly £30,000 for an inside single cabin. The standard daily rate for a cruise ship was well under £100, so sixty-six days with added luxury might come to something over £6,000. Clearly people were covering their own costs and I forgot all about it.

Until, of course, I saw the price start to come down … and down. At £7,000 I started to become interested. As the sailing date became imminent, I suggest a mild panic may have set in. When the cost suddenly fell much lower with less than a month to go, I pounced.

Sad to say that during the first week on board, the one topic that bubbled contentiously just below the dining tables was the cost of everyone's ticket. People who had bought at the original offer price were horrified at the later discount. Matters got worse when it was uncovered that the ex-employees, stewardesses and the like, were travelling free.

It might be becoming obvious that I will never go sea cruising again. The weather was rough at the start and at the end, sufficient for me to abandon ship in Barcelona. Part of the forecastle was ripped from its foundation while sailing from Naples and seawater coursed down a first-class passageway and flooded cabins. I was continually bored with good conversation difficult to find. Many of the passengers were insurance widows. After days at sea, it was all a mad dash to arrange transport and get to see a port's hinterland in daylight. It could also take an age to get on and off by ship's boat at the smaller ports. Many passengers were content with anodyne coach trips. The best that could be said was that the extensive itinerary visited some unusual places and gave a view of where was worth a later return.

At a personal level, I was on holiday and hated the dressing up. Diner jackets were a preferred code for too many nights, often several in a row. After a while, I was offered a separate table in the dining room where the scruffs were accommodated.

One other complainant surprised me for he was the richest man on the boat: Jack Hayward or *Union Jack* for his patriotism. He was well into his seventies and preferred to slough around in casual gear. He made his fortune through his father's business and a deep association with Bermuda. As well as a home in Freeport, he owned a farm in Sussex and in Scotland was Laird of Dunmaglass, a 14,000 acre estate near Inverness. The *Sunday Times* rich list placed him at 125th in Britain. He owned Wolverhampton Wanderers football club in his home town, bought Lundy Island in the Bristol Channel for the National Trust and funded three international racing yachts, *Great Britain I, II* and *III*.

Naturally, Jack Hayward had the largest suite on the *Victoria*. I don't know how much he paid for it. It seemed that, every few days while at sea, he would throw an open party in his rooms for passengers with whom he had shared a table. I never eat with him, but I did hear that he provided copious champagne and canapés. Shamefully, I gate crashed one event; there was no security. I was the only one apart from him who was tieless. He welcomed me kindly, made sure I had a drink then left me to my own devices.

At various stages of the voyage, celebrities were flown in to give talks in the ship's theatre come cinema. I have to admit some of the 'celebrities' were unknown to me, but I did slump into a deck chair next to one of them.

'You're Murray Walker,' I said. 'I claim my prize of a free ride in your taxi.'

'Oh, God,' he groaned, 'I'm supposed to be incognito. Now you're going to blab it all over the ship.'

'Well, to be fair, your straw hat isn't much of a cover. And you are holding a steering wheel.'

'Don't talk to me,' he said, so I didn't. A few minutes later he grumbled off.

Walker was still in his prime, providing television commentary of live Formula One races for the BBC. He gave an excellent talk which echoed his screen personality: animated enthusiasm, authority, extreme knowledge of his subject and comical blunders. There was no one connected with motor sport whom he didn't know and he had a disrespectful story about all of them.

I waved at him from the audience, but he didn't respond.

I also attended an entertaining session given by Sir Bernard Ingram who, ten years before, in 1990, had finished eleven years as Margaret Thatcher's Press secretary. In the course of a long civil service career, Ingham was also secretary to Barbara Castle, Robert Carr, Maurice Macmillan, Lord Carrington, Eric Varley and Tony Benn, so he knew a story or two. As a pugnacious and increasingly opinionated master of the black arts of spin, Ingham was also involved in every major political drama of the eighties. His ludicrously bushy eyebrows became a feature of television at that time.

After the talk, I found Ingham slumped at a dark, secluded bar table with a large glass in front of him.

'Glad that's over?' I asked.

'I'm just getting old,' he said, 'and I don't much like boats, but the money's good.'

'I'll piss off if you want,' I offered.

He shook his head and I ordered replacement drinks. We shared some background as we both were trained journalists, he at Bradford, me at Darlington. We talked about the old days, about the drop in journalistic standards, about criticism of him for his part in moving Thatcher to a more presidential style of UK leader without the constitutional safeguards. We may have talked for sixty minutes when he eventually groaned and decided on bed.

A few days later, Pam Ayres read 'some of me poetry', but I didn't get to meet her, surrounded as she always was by adoring lady fans with their pens at the ready.

*Victoria* was sold by P&O shortly afterwards and, as the *Mona Lisa*, got stuck right in front of St Mark's Square in Venice in heavy fog. Her company went bankrupt and she was chartered as a hotel ship in Doha, Qatar, for the Asian Games. As *Oceanic II*, she covered for the cruiser *Sea Diamond* which sank off Santorini in Greece. She then became a scholar ship and, later, as the *Mona Lisa* again, grounded in the Irbe Strait while leaving Riga. After a spell as floating accommodation at Squamish, Canada, for the Winter Olympics in 2010 and as a luxury floating hotel, named *Veronica*, at Duqm, Oman, she was laid up for two years. In 2015, she was towed by a tug to the ship breaking yard in Alang, India, were she was beached at high tide and scrapped.

# PAUL DAVID 'BONO' HEWSON

Irish singer songwriter and activist, U2 rock band

# SIR GEORGE IVAN 'VAN THE MAN' MORRISON

Irish musician

*Bono, 2017.* Daniel Hazard.   *Van Morrison, 2015.* ArtSiegal.

'Street cred' is an important part of being a respected parent. Money cannot buy 'cred' status. To seek it, to try to learn its ways, is a transparent act leading to teenage disdain. It follows that to have one's 'cred' acknowledged, one has to arrive, as it were, by accident. It also follows that the point of arrival may not be understood at the time, or even recognised, by the parent.

I had some weeks in the sun following a chance encounter. It was greeted by a shriek from my daughter.

'You ate Bono's sausage,' she yelled, so excited that she almost ran into the street to share the news.

For a while I wondered whether social services might soon knock on the door. What sort of offence had I committed? Was a dog involved? Might it even be a matter for the police? I was instructed to sit down and recount my story in the smallest detail. The trouble was it had occurred on a Guiness-fuelled rugby weekend in Dublin. Events and sequences were more than a little hazy, but the core fact was true and decidedly out of the bag. I had, indeed, eaten Bono's sausage.

My brother suggested a weekend away to watch an international rugby match between Ireland and Wales at the Lansdown Park stadium. I had not been to Dublin in years, not since, I think, that I lived for six months in Bangor in County Down as a boy and had made a couple of trips there by train. That's wrong: I did go for a couple of days which were spent in a smoke-filled room with seized windows auditing a strike at a local factory.

I flew from Edinburgh and was met by my brother standing at the bottom of the arrival escalator holding two pints of the black stuff. It was getting towards lunchtime and we had an appointment with a friend of my brother's in a pub in O'Connell Street. This friend was an older, slightly disreputable, character, a life-long journalist, who was known in every bar in town and took his drinking seriously. The conversation was wild and unstructured, regularly interrupted by passers-by as they stumbled into our table and offered drinks and stories.

I remember passing out single roses as we wandered along the Quays. Our broad purpose was to seek out some of the pubs made famous by James Joyce like *Davy Byrne's*, *The International* and *The Oval*, *J M Cleary's* (also in deference to Michael Collins) and, of course *Mulligan's* and possibly one or two others.

By seven o'clock, we planned to be at the Guiness Brewery in St James's Gate. The free party for rugby's great and good was a noted part of every Irish international weekend. We had no tickets. As we approached the door, my brother fell behind me so that I was alone when stopped by the attendant.

'Ticket, Sir,'

My brother rushed up and spoke urgently into the man's ear.

'For the love of God man, do you not recognise the greatest Number Eight never to have played for Ireland and only because of his terrible injuries?'

The guard assessed me. I tried to look large and menacing and injured.

'Sorry, my boy,' he said and stood aside. 'Didn't recognise you at first. Apologies. Enjoy yourself.' I mumbled dignified thanks.

And we were in. The bars in the brewery were laden with ready-poured glasses of draught Guiness. Teams of staff worked behind the scenes to fill spaces emptied. Smart young girls wafted around with trays of sandwiches, pork pies and, for some reason, vol-au-vents. It was like the Hall of Valhalla full of revered Welsh and Irish Valkyries. We were surrounded by several dozen famous faces, anyone of which would have demanded a space in this book if only I had spoken to them.

But then I did, if only a few. My brother used to play centre for Newport High School and was acquainted with international players in the early 1970s like David Burcher. I well remember a resplendent Gareth Edwards in sweeping black cape, surrounded by acolytes, walking by the pitch shouting, 'Give it to Heal on the burst'. He was recognised and that's how, much later, we ended sitting in a pub listening to and robustly joining in a legendary evening of local song.

My brother nudged me and I moved to prop him up.

'No,' he explained, pointing. 'There. There. It's *Van the Man*.'

And it was.

Van saw me looking at him. I waved and gave him a thumbs up. He did the same and raised his glass in salute. I did the same.

'I didn't realise that you knew him,' said my brother, slightly in awe. I was slow enough not to deny it.

Van Morrison was already world famous for songs like *Gloria* and *Brown Eyed Girl*. In his career he had more that forty albums in the UK Top 40. He has two Grammy Awards, a Brit Award, an American Lifetime Achievement Award and inductions into both the Rock and Roll and Songwriters Halls of Fame. He was knighted in 2016.

I have no idea where we slept that night, but I do remember presenting ourselves for breakfast the next day, the match day. I had been introduced through work to a colleague in Dublin who had found two tickets for me. And, kindness itself, he threw in an invitation to a pre-game feast at, a shaky memory says, The Royal Dublin Golf Club. It was a prestigious and slightly formal affair. We were handed ties at the door.

Convention was that you sat next to someone that you did not know or knew only slightly. There were lots of empty single spaces and I settled into one. A large plate of sausage, bacon, eggs, black pudding, tomatoes and fried bread appeared. Drink was a choice between tea and Guiness and I wasn't in the mood for tea. It was kill or cure.

I got chatting to the young man on one side with black hair swept high and back.. His name was Paul, 'but people usually call me Bono,' he offered. We shook hands.

'So, what do you do?' I asked.

'I sing and play guitar in a rock and roll band.' He paused. 'I also write songs.'

'Gosh,' I said. 'This may be embarrassing for you and for me, but I'm not very up on popular bands. Would I know the name?'

'U2. We've been going about four years. I also play the guitar, but I'm not very good at it.'

I shook my head slowly. 'Sorry, but I don't think I know the band.'

To be fair to me, U2 was in its infancy. The band was definitely on the teenage radar, but was nowhere the legend it became. Four years after I met Bono, U2 performed at the Live Aid benefit concert at Wembley Stadium before a crowd of 72,000 and a worldwide television audience of 1.5 billion people. U2 has won twenty-two Grammy Awards and two Golden Globe awards for Best Original Song (*The Hands That Built America* in 2003 and *Ordinary Love* in 2014). In 2005, Bono was inducted into the Rock and Roll Hall of Fame. He has also received many personal awards for his international charitable campaigns and is renowned for his philanthropy and activism for human rights and social justice. These activities have led to the French Legion of Honour, an honorary knighthood, the annual Man of Peace award, and the US Presidential Medal of Freedom.

It was in the area of poverty and AIDS in Africa, particularly Ethiopia, that Bono and I spent our time talking over breakfast. We shook hands again after one mildly heated exchange.

'Interesting ideas,' he said.

'I wish you well with the good fight … and the band,' I responded. 'Do you not want that sausage? Seems a shame to waste it.'

He nodded agreement and I forked it off his plate.

Of course, I cannot be sure, but to this day, I don't think I have knowingly heard any of U2's music, but I have read frequently that Bono has made a difference in the world.

I also don't remember much of the match which I felt was a little unexciting. I think it was 1980 with Ireland winning 21-7 and breaking a long run of Welsh successes. I remember Brian O'Driscoll scored a try.

Even today, when a new visitor of the right age and sex comes to my home, I am often introduced as the man who ate Bono's sausage. The news is still received with appropriate shock and awe.

Yeahh!!!

# JEFFREY OWEN HAWKES

South African golfer

# ANTHONY ALASTAIR JOHNSTONE

Zimbabwean golfer and Sky Sports commentator

*Jeff Hawkes, 2010.*
Pvt Pauline.

*Tony Johnstone, 2012.*
Pvt Pauline.

Outside the sun was burning. In my office in Main Street, Johannesburg, the air conditioning meant there was a slight chill. After a busy start, it was a slow late morning and I was beginning to think about lunch, may be a kingklip curry or a couple of lamb chops done to a pink turn, both options available across the road in the Carlton Centre. Perhaps, a colleague would ring and suggest somewhere altogether new.

The phone did buzz, but it was reception. There was a gentleman without an appointment asking to see me. His name was Jeff Hawkes. The name sounded familiar, but I couldn't place it. South Africa in the early 1980s was a bit like that. Diaries were more flexible; no waiting two weeks for a date. There was still an element of frontier in amongst the button down shirts of American business. My secretary had gone shopping, it was her mother's birthday next week.

'I'll be down in a few minutes,' I confirmed and began the first of two golfing 'personal moments'.

Jeff, about thirty, all sun-browned and healthy, pale blue open neck shirt and white Chinos, big smile, confident and a ready right hand. He was leaning, legs casually crossed, by the metal cabinet where employees could check in their handguns when they arrived for work.

'Outdoor worker,' I thought. 'Sportsman? Ahh, that Jeff Hawkes.' A professional golfer on the European tour, he had just been part of a ten-man team representing Rest of the World under the captaincy of Greg Norman in the Hennessy Cognac Cup. A team from Great Britain and Ireland had played and caused an apartheid stir in the British Press.

We shook hands.

'Is this a quick one, Jeff,' I asked, 'or do you want to come up to my office?'

I was IBM South Africa's Communications Manager, a catch all title that included marketing, press relations, employee communications and a number of odd jobs suitable for an assignee from the UK who was not embroiled in local politics.

'Let's start indoors, Chris' and so we soon sat side by side in some easy chairs, machine coffee rejected.

Jeff was on a one-man mission to get some more financial security into the South African professional golfing scene. While the local tour was popular, players had to last the expensive European season to have a chance of making ends meet. There was intense competition. Even the best of the bunch, Gary Player apart, had unsure lives. Surprise to tell, corporate South Africa had not seen the opportunity and stepped up. Jeff had seen the gap in the market and was starting his agency pitch with me. He had heard of my sporting interest through friends of friends in Zimbabwe.

His product for the day was Tony Johnstone, born in 1956 in Bulawayo. Tony was one of the younger, up and coming players, recently turned professional and who had just won the Portuguese Open. He was a reasonable bet for future stardom, but at the moment needed stability as he developed his game.

'How about an annual sponsorship for Tony?'

'What's the offer?'

'A set number of days golfing with clients, individual training sessions, a few motivational talks at major company events, although he's never done one before, name to be freely used, carry the company logo on some piece of kit to be decided...'

'What's in it for you?'

'Nothing, immediately. I might make a business out of this and look for an introductory cut, but for now I need a little success like any startup. Getting Tony taken on by a big firm would help set me up.'

'And working with Tony would be a gamble. He may get stability, but he may not win. We would have to be careful about associating with failure.'

'Annual renewable contract. No penalty breaks. He has just won the Portuguese.' Jeff mentioned a fee. It was lower than I expected.

'I don't play golf, just a few rounds for laughs with friends. I don't know Tony or his reputation. If we were interested, it would all depend on his personality, how he would fit in with big men in big corporations.'

'Agreed. How about a provisional meeting with you to see whether you are prepared to put his name forward?'

And, so, I met Tony over a beer in a plush out-of-town golf club, only he took a soft drink, with Jeff trying hard to steer the conversation without being too pushy. What a pleasant young man Tony was, nervous a little, of course, fresh faced, open, interested, knew when to keep quiet, when to assert his sporting authority.

'Jeff says you hardly play,' said Tony. 'I can always give you some tuition away from the public eye.'

'I'll pass, Tony,' I said, 'but thank you for the offer. My life's full enough at the moment without hours getting fit on a golf course.'

I then told him of a tiny golfing venture of my own. My rented home was in the suburb of Bryanston with just under an acre or so of ground. I had recently had some fun putting in a very amateur thirteen hole chip and put course (there was no room for any more) for my children. We used baked bean tins placed in holes in the tough Kikuyu grass and little flags with numbers as markers. There were plenty of natural hazards like trees, dogs and the swimming pool. The children had developed a course card and decided on the par performances.

One of my favourite holes in the garden was by a lemon tree which always seemed to carry fruit and gave an extra fresh-picked dash to gin and tonic.

'Hey, I'll come and play. That sounds like fun,' said Tony.

I was embarrassed.

'That's not what I was hinting at, Tony,' I said. 'I really don't think it's suitable for you and it's not necessary to further our contract discussions. It would be awful if you hurt your wrist in the rough.'

'No, we get on. I'd like to.'

This second golfing personal moment is about Tony Johnstone, European championship winner, giving personal advice to my children as we played a few rounds with my few third-hand clubs one Saturday afternoon in my garden, putting into sunken tin cans.

The man to persuade to take Tony on was IBM's marketing director, Tony Dry, an occasional and serous lunchtime drinking companion. I think he was often pleased to get away from the executive floor and his sales teams and meet me for a different sort of conversation. I led him into the plan slowly, talking about how pleasant it would be if he could pull a serious golfer out of a hat to interest his top clients and, of course, get out of the office more.

He almost bit my hand off and even offered to cover the cost.

The relationship between the two Tonys lasted several years, long after I left South Africa to return to the UK. Tony won six times in Europe and finished a career best seventh on the Tour Order of Merit in 1992 when he won the British PGA Championship. He also won seventeen times on the South African tour.

Tony was noted for his excellent short game and topped the European Tour's short game statistics in 1998, 1999 and 2000. I like to think that the training opportunity I provided in Bryanston had a part of play in that.

In 2004, Tony, living in Sunningdale, near Windsor in England, was diagnosed with multiple sclerosis. Fingers crossed, he appears to have put his MS into remission using a revolutionary drug. Jeff Hawkes lives nearby in Bracknell.

# RONALD EDMUND HUTTON

## English professor of history at Bristol University

Taking a research degree, particularly in the sciences, can mean disappearing into a darkened room or a locked laboratory for three years or even as many as ten. Colleagues are few and those that stay the course are similarly minded. The researcher is often on the path to become a world expert in their solitary slice of knowledge. Who can debate with them?

Life for the historian may be very different. The knowledge is out there, scattered and occasionally hard to find. Research is not at a workbench, but on the road (or used to be before the internet took away the fun and much of the skill) and, despite the many contacts, is often lonely.

*Ronald Hutton, 2002.* Evan Jones.

And, yet, it sometimes seems that everyone has always been an expert in your chosen subject.

As befits a PhD student delving into the felt hat industry over four hundred years, I kept meticulous notes during my time at Bristol University of my contacts and various sources. Each claim and example needed a footnote so that those who were to check my work or follow in my footsteps knew where to start.

Here's a flavour. I visited fifteen universities, over sixty research institutions (a few abroad by email) and called on five of them for over ten financial grants, twenty local societies (mostly to give talks which altogether amounted to over eighty), three heavily-used internet chat groups, one hundred and fourteen genealogists who claimed hatters among family members, forty-four academic experts from all walks of life, and I read some two hundred and fifty books and academic collections. Behind all that, I had two supervisors, Doctors Evan Jones and Richard Sheldon, and was forever grateful to Doctors Jonathan and Dylis Harlow, who gave me food, shelter, advice and support at their home in Winterbourne.

I was interested to see how hierarchical university life was. I was in my sixties, well used if intolerant of corporate life. I am sure there was a controlling structure behind the scenes at Bristol, but much of my time was free with no set hours other than suggestions for visits, meetings, books and chapter reviews with my supervisors.

For instance, I hardly met the professor of history at Bristol, Ronald Hutton. Hutton was born in 1953, six years earlier than me. When I did see him, he was always a kindly man. With his slight build, shoulder-length hair, waistcoats and colourful tie pieces, he was as unexpected from a distance as his chosen subjects. Born in India of a colonial family with part Russian ancestry, Hutton had an early and practical interest in archaeology. He won a scholarship at Pembroke College, Cambridge and went on to Oxford where he gained a doctorate, supervised by Hugh Trevor-Roper, and took a fellowship at Magdalen College. Initially, Hutton concentrated on the English civil war.

We first met in the street outside a Bristol University building. There was a pause. I felt, perhaps as the older man, that I should introduce myself.

'I want to congratulate you,' he said, slightly formal and stilted, 'for the extensive work you have done in taking your research to the villages around Bristol and in the city. It does great credit to you and to the university.'

I thanked him and, that said, we parted.

In 2011, I gave a talk in an academically competitive setting at Cardiff University. I noticed Hutton was also on the agenda, speaking on his, by now, preferred subject, 'Paganism'. I sat in the front row and wished I hadn't. The subject was difficult for me. With my business background, I struggled to come to terms with discourses about fairies and modern, but active, witchcraft. It's my personal issue, of course. I accept that. My talk later, *Manufacturing myth: Madness, riot and cowboys: Secrecy and conjecture in the hat industry* didn't go particularly well either.

Hutton has written about twenty books and often appears on television and radio dealing with English folklore, pre-Christian religion and contemporary Paganism. His books include, for example, *The Triumph of the Moon, The History of Modern Pagan Witchcraft* 1999; *Shamans and Witches, Druids and King Arthur*, 2003; and *Blood and Mistletoe, the History of the Druids in Britain*, 2009.

One reviewer commented, 'Predictably, Hutton finds himself defending his position on two fronts. Neo-pagans, clinging to the notion that their beliefs are part of an ancient nature religion, and radical feminists upholding the idea of a matriarchal society (which Hutton finds 'rather delightful'), scorn Hutton's refreshingly cheerful acceptance that there seems little evidence for either of these. And his less unbuttoned colleagues shake their heads at his optimism about Druidry and other 'alternative spiritualities' as valid contemporary religions.'

The last time I met, Hutton, I was standing at a urinal. He came in and took position near me. We said nothing. It wasn't that I am naturally shy, although I can be, but he offered no recognition. I really didn't have anything to say, so I didn't. He left first.

I didn't attend my graduation, fed up with ceremony and fearing a sweaty hall full of undergraduates and their parents, so I missed my chance of a final farewell.

I found I agreed directly with Hutton on one matter when I read, 'My colleagues would kill me for saying this, but historians are increasingly conscious of the fact that we can't write history. What we can write about is the way people see history and think history happens.' My support for this approach, without knowing Hutton's view at the time, was a constant bone of contention with fellow researchers.

I have been indulgent. The point I wanted to reach was to recognise a few of those from the long, previous list of expert contacts while I dealt with my PhD. A number had earned their place in *Wikipedia* and had directly influenced me for good or ill and so could have taken a chapter in this book.

Tim Carter specialised in the prevention of occupational health risks, working in industry and government. For fifteen years, he was the senior doctor in the Health and Safety Executive. Recently, he advised on transport safety, especially the health of seafarers. Tim and I discussed at length the occupational health effects of the practices of the early felt hatting industry.

Jill Cook, Fellow of he Society of Antiquaries of London, is a British Museum curator and the acting Keeper of the Department of Britain, Europe and Prehistory. She curates the collection of European Prehistory and is a specialist in the Ice-Age and the archaeology of human evolution. Jill and I collaborated on a talk on Henry Christy, of the hatting dynasty, at the Museum.

Dr Clive Field is Honorary Research Fellow in Modern History at the University of Birmingham and also an Honorary Research Fellow at the University of Manchester. Until 2006, he was Director of Scholarship and Collections at the British Library, He has a particular interest in the social history of Methodism. He advised me, and we often disagreed, on my thesis chapter on Methodism and the South Gloucestershire hatters. I also took advice on the subject from the Rev Dr David Hart, the Superintendent Minister of the Bristol and South Gloucestershire Circuit.

Dr. Negley Harte (with a soft 'g', Chris) is an Emeritus Senior Lecturer in the history department at University College London (UCL). He is interested in textile production and consumption in the sixteenth to nineteenth centuries. We met at a pub in Wiltshire to discuss my research and whether and how I should take a degree.

Stuart Peachey is a British historian specialising in the English Civil War and the history of food and clothing. He has produced many works on these and other subjects and is compulsively active in living history. I met Stuart and his small team at his home south of Bristol, surrounded by practical proofs of his speciality, where we discussed dyeing and manufacturing techniques in the making of felt hats.

Thom Richardson was Deputy Master and Head of Collections and Keeper of the Armour and Oriental Collections at the Royal Armouries Museum in Leeds. Thom advised me on the use of felt as an underwear for medieval armour. We also discussed the use of felt sheets on board sailing warships to catch deadly wooden splinters sent flying by enemy cannonballs.[17]

Cynthia Rosers was a devoted advocate for preserving African-American history. She gave freely of her time over the internet to explain Jamaican slave

---

17 Burn, James Dawson, *A Glimpse at The Social Conditions of The Working Classes during the early part of the Present Century, Trade Strikes and their Consequences to the People who may be immediately Connected with them with Reflections upon Trades' Unions and their Management* (London Heywood 1868).

history and investigated with me the influence of felt hats on the trade in humans.

Keith Snell is an academic historian who holds a personal chair as Professor of Rural and Cultural History at the University of Leicester. He directed me in detail on the 1691 Settlement Act and its effect of village apprenticeships.[18]

David Vincent is Emeritus Professor of Social History at The Open University, and Visiting Professor at Keele University. He is the author or editor of sixteen books on British and European social history and, as such, is an expert on James Burn, a nineteenth-century author on social working conditions with a particular emphasis on the felt hatting industry.

Thank you to everyone and to those not mentioned.

---

18 Snell, K D M, *Annals of the Labouring Poor, Social Change and Agrarian England 1660-1900* (CUP 1985).

# ALUN ARTHUR GWYNNE JONES
## Baron Chalfont, Welsh journalist and politician

Most of the famous people I met, those 'famous' enough to have an entry in *Wikipedia*, carried no particular aura. Were it not for their ceremonial costume or the appropriateness of the place of meeting, one might otherwise have passed them by in the street without a further glance. Just a couple projected their presence, made you feel in that personal moment that you were the undoubted centre of their attention or, in the right circumstance, that if they chose to lead then you would follow. Perhaps it was a trick they possessed that could be turned on and off cynically and at will. But then again, it could have been chemistry, some variant of asexual love at first sight when, until the warts were uncovered, you were swept off your feet.

*Alun Chalfont.*

My first experience of the phenomena was with the prosaically named Alun Gwynne Jones, born in 1919, the son of a miner and a teacher from the Monmouthshire coalfields in what was later called 'modest circumstances'. His later biographies downplayed his early life. He told me that 'quite often we were pretty poor, especially when a strike was on'.

Gwynne Jones, when I met him, was Baron Chalfont of Llantarnam, a life peerage created in 1964 so that he could join the Labour government of Harold Wilson as Minister of State for Foreign and Commonwealth Affairs. He had previously been a distinguished defence correspondent for *The Times* for three years where he had caught Wilson's eye.

We met early in 1974 when I worked for IBM in the UK as editor of their employee newspaper distributed to their 15,000 or so staff. The American company was building the strength and diversity of its UK Board in an attempt to prove British commitment when opportunities for large-scale and sensitive government contracts increased. Gwynne Jones had just been appointed as a non-executive director of IBM UK under the chairmanship of the 3rd Earl of Cromer of the Baring banking family, a former governor of the Bank of England and also the British ambassador to the United States. It was truly a time for hugging the establishment.

When I suggested the interview with Gwynne Jones on the grounds that IBM's UK employees should know more about their directors, my management were taken aback by the audacity of the idea. There were many meetings, from which I was mostly excluded, as the request made its way to rarefied heights. Responsibility for any failure was passed carefully up the chain. The eventual approval came from Cromer and Eddie Nixon, the company's UK managing director. The process, and the final agreement, left me in no doubt that if I was ever to get anywhere in life it would be outside IBM. The eventual break took another twenty years although I offered my resignation several times. I regard the delay as one of my life's failures.

Chalfont, as an experienced journalist and politician, was relaxed about the interview, indeed he was looking forward to it. I was, as he told me immediately, the only company employee he had met outside of the Board. He was looking for a two-way exchange of information and views.

The interview took place at his tastefully decorated home in west London on a sunny morning, somewhere near the river, I think, perhaps Chelsea? Tea and shortbread biscuits were ready. He settled in his favourite armchair with a backdrop of memoirs, biographies and modern history books overflowing the shelves. I perched on a deep sofa with my notebook balanced on my crossed knee and we started to chat.

Chalfont asked me if I was under orders and whether my copy would be scrutinised. I joked that, once approval had been given for the interview, management seemed to have lost interest. I wasn't sure who would be checked up on in the end, him or me. I suspected we both had opinions which may not fit the official line.

He was a confident man with an easy way of engaging which made me feel that my views were important and appreciated. We disagreed on a number of political matters, but, as I pointed out, we were not there to understand my opinions.

I was keen to know how he had got from his miner's two-up, two-down to the School of Slavonic Studies at the University of London. Luck, hard work, talent, teachers who cared and a desire to get out into the world, he offered.

I wish I had asked him more about his military service. Possibly, he manoeuvred me away. At the outbreak of war, he joined the South Wales Borderers as a lieutenant. He fought in Burma for almost four years, part alongside the Welsh poet Alun Lewis. In 1944, Lewis was found shot in the head, after shaving and washing near the officers' latrines, with his revolver in his hand. Despite it being a clear suicide, a court of inquiry charitably concluded that he had tripped and that the shooting was an accident.

Chalfont stayed in the Army and was promoted to major in 1953. He took part in a series of ambushes against communist insurgents during the Malayan Emergency and received a Military Cross 'for gallantry and relentless determination over eighteen months in jungle operations'. Chalfont was awarded the OBE in 1961 when he retired with the honorary rank of lieutenant colonel.

He was the spokesman for the attempt by the Labour government to divest Britain of the Falklands Islands. He travelled there to assess local feeling and was persuaded that they wished to remain British. He believed that one day the islanders might choose Argentine sovereignty.

Chalfont resigned from the Labour Party in the early 1970s on a 'decision of personal and political principle'. He looked in vain for a realignment of the radical left. In 1979, he defected to support Margaret Thatcher at the general election.

Of particular interest was Chalfont's burgeoning TV and writing career. He interviewed many world leaders for his popular programme. The one that he most regretted missing, he told me, was President Salvador Allende of Chile who committed suicide in his palace in 1973 while surrounded by CIA-led troops. Chalfont's books included works on Montgomery of Alamein and the Sultan of Brunei.

My two pages on Chalfont appeared in IBM's newspaper without a hitch or unkind comment. What no one from the company knew was that, a month later, I had lunch with Chalfont, 'call me Alun, please', at the House of Lords. I was introduced to a dozen or so famous peers, none of whom talked to me for long enough to get their own chapter in this book.

Gwynne Jones died a month after his one hundredth birthday in 2020.

# NIGEL KENNEDY

## English violinist

Nigel Kennedy is the ageing *enfant terrible* of classical music. Frequently in trouble with the establishment, he increasingly dressed in battered garments, majoring on leather and plastic, and extreme haircuts and brought his left-wing views as a committed socialist onto the performing stage.

*Nigel Kennedy, 2010*. Hans Westbeek, Flickr.

In 1991, the Controller of BBC Radio 3, John Drummond, described Kennedy as 'a Liberace for the nineties' and objected to his 'ludicrous' clothes and 'self-invented accent'.

Yet Nigel Kennedy could play a sublime violin and had record and CD sales for which most professional performers would give an eye tooth.

And then, for a long while, he gave it all up.

Kennedy, born in Brighton in 1956 was a child prodigy, a pupil at the Yehudi Menuhin School of Music, aged seven. He studied at the Juilliard School in New York, helping to pay for his studies by busking. At sixteen, he was invited by jazz violinist Stephane Grapelli to appear with him at New York's Carnegie Hall. Kennedy's recording of Vivaldi's *The Four Seasons* in 1989 sold over two million copies.

In 1992, Kennedy quit classical music and chose other genres: a cover of Jimi Hendrix's *Fire*; in 2000, *Riders on the Storm: The Doors Concerto*; and also joined the rock group *The Who* at the Royal Albert Hall, and then followed with several tracks with Kate Bush and Sarah Brightman and an exploration of Klezmer, the instrumental musical tradition of the Ashkenazi Jews of Central and Eastern Europe, with the Polish jazz band *Kroko*.

Kennedy returned to the Proms in 2008 after a twenty-one year absence and again in 2013 when he performed *The Four Seasons* with a group of young Palestinian musicians.

According to Michael Church in *The Independent*, in the first movement, 'Spring', Kennedy 'swerved off course with a flurry of bird tweets followed by a jazz riff from his bassist; the staccato chords of the next movement were decorated by a microtonal Arabic riff from one of the guest players'. Near the end of the concert, the BBC removed the violinist's attribution of apartheid to Isreal from the television broadcast, but were not quick enough for a cut to the live radio performance.

This was the man I met about 1988, just for a minute of so. One of the pleasures of my job was arranging sponsorship for classical music concerts around the country. This performance by Kennedy, of course the evening's star, was one of a series with the Bournemouth Symphony Orchestra (BSO), whose management I knew well.

Usually, I was well in the background at these events, but on this occasion I was invited onto the stage when the audience had cleared and there was Kennedy. We shook hands politely although I am not sure he really understood who I was and what was my role. In these situations, I am not usually at all stuck for words, being well used to providing an acceptable humorous bumble.

What I actually managed was one of my most embarrassing performances, mindless and without forethought. I congratulated Kenndy on his playing and conjectured, to bemusement all around, whether because of his loud foot stamping at crucial moments he might consider bringing a personal square of carpet on stage with him, exotically coloured to suit his personality.

'It could become a trademark,' I offered, failing to stop digging my personal hole. I was carefully moved on and, after a short reflection, fled.

I called the managing director of the BSO the next morning to apologise for my lapse in common sense.

'We all have our bad day,' he said. 'Kennedy didn't mention it, but then his head is usually somewhere else.'

# PATRICK 'MAXIE' LANE

## English sculptor, artist and author

Back in the 1970s, the Chestnut Tree pub on the Weyhill Road near Andover was what you might expect for a roadhouse of the period. I had recently joined the local newspaper as a reporter and was travelling back from a job at the Army garrison at Tidworth with Charlie Green, the resident photographer. Charlie knew all the watering holes in the area and had decided it was his duty to introduce them all to me in a short a time as possible.

*Maxie Lane.*

Around the walls of the pub were about a dozen cheaply framed charcoal drawings, obviously quickly done, but with the eye and line of a good artist. I asked the landlord whose work they were.

He gave a big sigh. 'They're all Maxie Lane,' he said. 'I've got more than I can deal with. He never has any money and then persuades me to take a drawing for a pint. I frame them and hang them on the walls to recoup my money. I've got no more space and they're not selling well enough.'

'How much do you charge for them?'

'Three quid will do it to cover the pint and the frame. Take your pick.'

So I did and the drawing of a young daughter, probably Lisa, still hangs on the wall of my current home.

I first met Maxie Lane when he appeared at the Andover magistrates' court, charged with indecent exposure. He had tried to buy a drink in what passed for an upper class bar in the Star & Garter Hotel in the centre of town. Maxie was barred for not wearing a tie. He told me that he felt that the rejection was as much to do with him personally and his record. He hated authority in most of its forms.

'Bloody snobs. If people have these silly rules, they should always have a set of ties behind the bar,' he declared.

Maxie found himself a tie and went back. The trouble was he had nothing else on.

I missed his later arrest for being, drunk, I think, and sitting on the pavement with his feet in the High Street gutter and wearing a Father Christmas outfit. It was a particularly hot June day.

Maxie's most famous brush with the law brought him national fame. He was with friends or family in the upstairs room of a Chinese restaurant, just by the courts. To my knowledge, the place had a mixed reputation. Maxie found the steak too tough and wasn't satisfied with the way his complaint was handled. The chainsaw he happened to have with him did get through the meat, and the table and a couple of chairs.

Whenever I talked to Maxie, he always stood up for the underdog. He had a deep loathing for the 'sloths' behind the rules and for the people who loved to apply them. His in-your-face attitude was always destined to land him in trouble. If you liked him, you tried to understand him. If you didn't, he was always a bad egg.

On Maxie's death, his children told the newspaper, 'He was a flawed diamond with many facets – artist, author, sculptor, a fun-loving hellraiser, bar-room brawler, prisoner, Army deserter, animal and nature lover, doting granddad and family man, totally unconventional and anti-establishment. He strongly believed in democracy and was actively opposed to corruption in high places.[19]

'He was incredibly strong and could bend and snap six-inch nails with his bare hands. He resembled a white Mike Tyson, but could punch even harder, in self-defence, if faced with danger or bullies.'

Maxi's notoriety led him to the Russell Harty and Esther Rantzen television chat shows. He also wrote two books of his early life, both of which are in an out-of-this-world style, but with 'breathtaking originality'. He revealed himself as a youthful inveterate thief.[20] Abandoned by his Irish tinker father to an aunt

---

19 *Andover Advertiser*, 2/5/2014.
20 Lane, Maxie, *Running* (Quartet Books 1978); *Sea-Running* (Macmillan 1978).

in Bristol when aged seven, he battled for survival in the city's slums. He spent his formative years in the Army, much of that time in prison or on the run, and in the worst of Britain's merchant fleet.

Maxie moved to the woods in Weyhill near the *Chestnut Tree* in the 1960s. It was there as a talented woodcarver that he made his main reputation. He mostly used wood from fallen trees, often elm, and his style was, as usual, unconventional.

I met him near his home among the trees, again with Charlie Green, where we were to view a long, wooden side table that was being made for a client. Charlie was most impressed, but Maxie was not happy. He walked around and around muttering. Finally, he heaved a sigh, grabbed an axe, turned it blade up and smashed it onto the wood surface. Charlie was aghast as the axe knocked out a large hole following the wood's contours. There was the finished article. Perfect.

Among his creations is what is thought to be the largest elm sculpture table in the world, *The Last Supper Table*, made from a 25-ton tree, which is on display at Furzey Gardens in the New Forest.

His daughter, Lisa, had a yard at Ludgershall for twenty years where she kept many of Maxie's unsold works, mainly tables and chairs. Lisa said the work was 'more than impressive furniture' and more like 'artifacts of a bygone era, akin to discovering a classic vintage car deserted in an old barn'.

Maxie spent hours buffing and polishing his best pieces and then travelled from pub to pub trying to sell them. I spent several pints in one place, trying to decide whether to buy a large table. Maxie said I could have it for £25, which was cheap, but was a week's wages. It was one of the worst decisions of my life when I said 'no'.

Maxie's work found its way into premier exhibitions and museums the world over. In his later life, fame brought interest from high-priced dealers. I saw recently that an elm centre table from the 1970s was for sale by Wick Antiques for £16,500.[21]

Maxie Lane died, aged 104, in 2014. He is survived by five sons, a daughter and many grandchildren and great-grandchildren.

---

21 Wick Antiques, just off Lymington High Street, https://wickantiques.co.uk.

# SIR EDWIN RONALD NIXON

Chief Executive, IBM UK; Chairman, Amersham International

# SIR LEONARD HARRY PEACH

Head of Personnel & Corporate Affairs, IBM UK; Chief Executive, NHS Management Board

*Eddie Nixon.* Daily Telegraph.

*Len Peach in the Sudan Canal Zone.* DizzleHistory.

In western Berlin on the Kurfürstendamm in the centre of the Breitscheidplatz lies a famous landmark called 'the hollow tooth'. It is the Kaiser Wilhelm Memorial Church, badly damaged in a bombing raid in 1943. The gutted spire, the tooth, has been retained and, in 1959, a new ground floor foyer and memorial chapel added with a separate belfry.

The original plan involved tearing down the old spire, but this was thwarted by a public outcry in which the ruined tower was deemed the 'heart of Berlin'.

Today, the walls of the new church are made of a concrete honeycomb with 21,292 glass inlays inspired by the glass in Chartres Cathedral. The predominant colour is deep blue with small areas of red, emerald green and yellow. Even this radical design did not gather local favour and the building is sometimes nicknamed *Lippenstift und Puderdose*, the lipstick and powder box, or the 'gasometer'.

Entering the church, the immediate effect is dramatic. Depending on the brightness of the weather outside, the blue can be overwhelming, making a moving, quasi-religious space. Opposite the altar is an organ with 5,000 pipes from which the sound of, usually, Bach sonatas resonate through the whole building. This was the principal reason for my visit. High above the altar, an eye-catching figure of the resurrected Christ hangs, made from brass alloy with a high copper content.

I groped along the central aisle, mesmerised and blinded by the all-around splendour, colour and sound, until I found a suitable chair at the beginning of a row and sat down.

From beneath me came an indignant squeak clearly from someone smaller than me. I stood up, turned to say 'sorry', and recognised in the gloom the flustered form of Eddie Nixon, the managing director of the company I worked for. He recognised me, too.

I moved away a few rows and rather than falling under the spell of the music considered what damage I might have done to my career in that personal moment.

Eddie and I were both in Berlin to attend what IBM called its 'Hundred PerCent Club', a jamboree for its most successful salesmen, those who had met or succeeded their annual quota. I was there as an internal journalist, to record the event, and to have a good time. It is worth emphasising this split in IBM's internal culture between the salesforce, those in manufacturing and those cerebral designers whose world was in research and spoke a different language. Most of the salesforce were graduates, many from Oxbridge. These were the people, usually male, who spread fear, uncertainty and doubt amongst their customers, and who were at the core of the company. No one ever got fired for buying IBM.

Eddie Nixon headed IBM's operations in the UK for over twenty years and we met many times, although I was always in a much junior role. He was highly respected inside and outside the company, becoming chairman and then chief executive, and was knighted in 1974. He left in 1988 to become chairman of Amersham International after it was spun off from Britain's nuclear industry in Margaret Thatcher's first privatisation. The share issue was almost twenty-five per cent oversubscribed and the price rocketed from by 48p to 142p in seconds. The company was later bought by GE and went into steep decline.

Nixon was a deputy lieutenant of Hampshire. He died in 2008.

Len Peach was another of IBM's knights. He was my director as head of Personnel and Corporate Affairs; he was also President of the Institute of Personnel Management. In 1985, Len was chosen by Norman Fowler, the Tory minister, to lead the new NHS Management Board after an initial spell as its Director of Personnel. The knighthood came in 1989. After a brief return to IBM, Peach became Chairman of the Police Complaints Authority and, later, Commissioner for Public Appointments. He died in 2016.

I had many 'personal moments' with Len Peach as befits an employee charged with employee communications. A favourite came after I interviewed a senior director for a profile in the company newspaper. He was a man I had met several times, gruff, forthright, in truth, a bully. I had recently published a separate interview with a fellow director who was not his best friend. It soon became apparent that there was great concern that my latest interviewee would be cast in a lesser light than his management competitor, not least because he was being interviewed second.

Within five minutes, I had been fired. We made it up and, a few minutes later, I was fired again. After a quarter of an hour, I had been fired seven times and even I realised that it was time to cut and run. We agreed to meet again in a couple of weeks time, but only if he decided to reinstate me.

What I had witnessed was a sad but evident break down, a long time in the making, but brought to the fore by the interview.

I called my line manager to explain what had happened and he called Len Peach. I told Len that I had an audio tape of the whole miserable affair and he asked for an urgent transcript. A few hours after its delivery, Len phoned me. I was not to worry. The director was taking a holiday. The follow-up interview was off indefinitely.

'Would I like a day at home?' I remember wondering what it would take to get two days to recover.

As it was a Friday, there seemed little point in joining the West London traffic too early. I was more concerned about how to fill two empty pages of the newspaper.

It was Len, a few years later, who called me at home in Edinburgh one early morning before I was dressed. I sat on my bed, watching the snow swirl outside my window and contemplating a bumpy winter flight to Leeds, as he asked if I would like to take a job in South Africa for two or three years. He asked me to meet him in Harrogate to discuss it at the side of a conference at which he was speaking. I drove down. His main point was that he didn't expect me to come back. He didn't even nibble the biscuit that came with his cup of tea.

As part of the internet research for this chapter, I came across a recent list, issued by IBM in the UK, titled 'The King and Honours'. It is a typical IBM list, ignorant of arrogance, that collects those employees named in New Year and Birthday honours lists either while employed or later ... 'IBM is acknowledged as having one of the most talented, capable and diverse workforces in the United Kingdom...' It reminded me of an Easter advert for a new IBM product issued many years ago: 'We're sorry to bore you with another miracle ...'

I was surprised how many of those named I had worked for, in some cases closely, or knew from regular meetings.

Sir Anthony Cleaver, chairman of IBM UK, was later Chairman of the United Kingdom Atomic Energy Authority, steering it through privatisation. He was knighted in 1992. Cleaver could have been on my 'personal moment' list for a distasteful event during a sponsored concert at the Sheldonian Theatre in Oxford.

I interviewed Sir John Fairclough who was a director of development before he moved to become Chief Scientific Adviser in the Cabinet Office (KBE, 1992). I worked at a distance for John Bache (OBE, 1982), director of manufacturing, who once rang me to tell me off for running a series of pictures of 'company' moustaches and asking readers to guess the owners. 'There is a line, Chris, and you have found it.'

James 'Jimmy' Miller (OBE, 1983), headed the Greenock manufacturing plant. We spent an excellent evening together in Berlin at the same event containing the unfortunate squashing of Eddie Nixon. We trailed around the local jazz clubs that he had ready listed. John McClelland (CBE, 1986) followed Jimmy at Greenock.

I worked directly for John McCracken (CBE, 1986) in Edinburgh when we both had grand titles covering Scotland and Northern England. He had a host of Scottish non-executive directorships and several worthy board memberships. But, I did beat him eight matches to two in our ongoing personal squash tournament.

Lastly, I worked for David Livermore, Southern General Manager in Basingstoke (OBE, 2008).

Surprisingly, the IBM honours list omits Sir Len Peach. And surely my old boss Nick Jonas, who retired from IBM to become chairman of the Hampshire NHS Trust with numerous wards and facilities named after him, received an honour?

# ANTHONY NOLAN

## Young sufferer from rare inherited blood disorder

This chapter is a subterfuge. I admit it. I never met Anthony Nolan, but I did meet the boy who was intended to be Nolan. In fact, I knew him well. He was my cousin.

Anthony Nolan was born in 1971 and died eight years later from Wiskott-Aldrich syndrome, a rare inherited blood disorder. His mother, Shirley Nolan, courageously and tirelessly campaigned for funds and then set up in 1974 a UK charity in her son's name and honour to manage and recruit stem cell donors. The charity, now a household name, moved from the Westminster Children's Hospital to its present offices, laboratory and research institute in the grounds of the Royal Free Hospital in north London.

In 2008, the charity set up the UK's first dedicated cord blood bank, allowing mothers to safely donate the blood from their umbilical cord and placenta after they gave birth and for later use in transplants. Today, Nolan's register has over 720,000 potential donors. Their university recruitment arm now operates in more than fifty universities worldwide.

In 2014, Anthony Nolan was the official charity partner for the London Marathon.

The family story is that Gregory Anthony Scott, the cousin and eighteen years younger than me, had the same disease as Nolan and that his mother, my aunt Dora, was first approached to be a figurehead for the charity campaign. Worn out by the constant travel from Somerset to London for his treatments, often experimental, and by other problems at home, Dora declined. Despite some pressure, she felt you would not have enough to give although thoroughly supporting the charity's objectives. Hence, Nolan became a household name and Scott is forgotten

Gregory was a spoiled child. I thought him difficult to get on with and not at all like the idyllic cherubs that disadvantaged and unfortunate children are all supposed to be. However, he was the apple of his mother's eye and was surrounded by toys and tolerance. My duties as godparent were non-existent and, considering my position on her religion, she was a more than devout Roman Catholic, I was a bizarre choice as godfather. The decision was taken out of my hands after I first refused. Dora was one of four sisters, including my mother, a formidable array when determined.

Dora married late, aged thirty-nine, to an Anglo-Indian bus driver called Walter who was eight years older than her. He was a kindly man, docile even, keen to do right. It was when the hereditary nature of Gregory's disease was revealed that it was also discovered that Walter had advanced syphilis. As he explained to me, in tears, he had once been with a prostitute in London many years before and had no idea he had caught the disease or of the long-lived consequences if untreated. One can imagine that from thereon there were regular recriminations both spoken and unspoken while Gregory hovered on the edge. Dora treated Walter at home, but that meant his agreement to retire to an attic bedroom each night at nine o'clock and to be locked in. He was still regularly fed his preferred and delicious home-cooked curries.

Gregory died at Queen Elizabeth Hospital in London in 1980, aged fifteen, after a wonder drug brought false hope. He was cremated in his home town of Taunton.

He was the boy who would have been Anthony Nolan.

Perhaps the centre of this chapter should be Dora who withstood so much and yet had so much humour. At one stage, she gave me all of her saved money because she was fearful that another member of her family would take it from her. My brother and I bought her her own house in later life so that she could find some peace.

Dora took up district nursing after the war and, in the 1950s, covered a large area of Somerset, based on Wiveliscombe, where I was born.[22] It seems she was known in every run-down cottage on every farm near every village in the county. She had an early black Ford Anglia and attacked the high-hedged, country lanes, always seemingly covered in primroses, without fear by assuming little oncoming traffic, but peeping her horn at every corner.

---

22 Heal, Chris *The Four Marks Murders,* Chapter 14, 'The Care of the Innocents' (C&S 2020, 2nd edition).

It was also a way of announcing her arrival. 'Peep. Nurse is here. Peep.'

Late in life, she showed me her maternity record book with over 2,000 entries, delivered at all hours, almost all single-handed, often by candlelight, while family members scattered for hot water and clean linen, or sat waiting on hard chairs with hands clenched in worry.

Dora reckoned she delivered about three babies a week for over fifteen years. 'They seemed to like two in the morning.'

One time, I put her to the test as we walked down a west Somerset High Street. Every child we passed, perhaps two dozen, said, 'Morning, nurse.' Two girls even curtsied. Dora named every one, their address, where they were born and what they were doing now. There was a wave and a personal comment for each young person.

'Forty-nine of my mothers were taken to hospital before the birth for complications,' she told me, with a heavy emphasis on the 'my'. I only lost eight babies on my own, apart from stillbirths, and two mothers. Two of those babies were my fault, but the families refused to make a complaint although I told them what happened.' Dora was always hard on herself.

No one had a phone. The eldest child was trained to cycle or run to the nearest shop, pub or rich house. Everyone had nurse's number prominently displayed. Often, she would slow the car to pick up the messenger trudging their way back up a hill to home. It feels now that I spent almost the whole of many summers as a boy in short trousers sitting beside her with her black labrador, Kelly, in the back, tongue hanging out of a window, as we drove to her appointments.

I don't know why I was there rather than with my parents, but I loved it. Every house, some none to clean with chickens strutting around the flag-stoned kitchens, had cake, home-baked biscuits and lemonade. While I waited, I would talk to the old people sitting in the sun on a bench near the porch or play with the children and their pets or help with the farm animals. Everywhere there were neat rows of healthy vegetables standing proud in the red earth.

Pregnancies and babies were the centre of Dora's life, then the chronically ill and people recovering from accidents and hospital operations, and, of course, the slowly dying. Her objective was to keep hospital beds available for the most needy. She didn't keep a log of deaths. The worst for me was the screams from the diabetics. In those days, in my imagination, the needles were four inches long, thick and very painful.

It seems like Dora never bought food. In the runner and broad bean seasons especially, my job was to place the gifts carefully on the back seat then, when we were out of sight, Dora would stop and I would move the vegetables, fruit and meat into the boot, out of sight, so as not to offend anyone and always leaving her 'special bag' uncovered. I discovered much later that the special bag was for the babies that didn't survive birth. The storage space was usually shared with skinned rabbits, a ham or two and joints of chicken.

When we came to the poorer families, often on the outskirts of a large village, I would select a load of food for redistribution. The one thing I couldn't stand was the smell of hare.

Dora was a natural and wicked storyteller and led her audience slowly through every revelation. Her tales often had a black side and many would not fit well with today's cautious sentiments. But she was honest and people already knew her innate kindness.

She told me one day of a frantic call about a young man who had been missing over night. He had mental health problems and was on suicide watch. She raced to the family farm and, after a brief discussion with a brother, drove to a local hilltop much visited by courting couples. They found the man dangling from a rope tied around a bough. He had died late the night before and was stiff from rigor mortis. Dora held the man's ankles to keep him still while the brother climbed the tree to cut the rope. As the body was released, Dora found herself staggering round the hill carrying the upright stiff corpse, fearful of letting go, waiting for the brother to catch up.

Dora once visited a dim cottage occupied by two elderly sisters. One of them had died during the day and was laid out on her bed, the room lit by a single candle. Dora checked the body over and moved to the kitchen for a cup of tea. She heard a noise behind her, turned, and there stood the 'dead' sister who had been woken by a noise. Apparently, she lived for another two years.

One routine visit to a pregnant woman turned into a nightmare as a slightly undersized baby was born. Then another. And another. It was a case of checking, snipping, washing and wrapping and moving on to the next. After two hours, Dora and the mother were exhausted. Dora placed the infants in the mother's arms. One, two, three, four and sat down in the rocking chair only to shoot bolt upright.

'I thought there were five. You've only got four. You did have five babies, didn't you?'

'I don't know,' wailed the mother. 'I thought I was only going to have one.'

Dora searched the room. A cry from the sofa led her to the fifth, hidden beneath a discarded blanket.

'I was sure it was five,' she told her audience.

So, this is a chapter that, perhaps, by my own rules, shouldn't be in this book. But, I weighed it, and decided that Gregory and Dora's story of life and death had earned its place.

# CHUKWUEMEKA ODUMEGWU OJUKWU
President of Biafra

# FREDERICK MCCARTHY FORSYTH
English novelist and journalist

*Chukwuemeka Odumegwu Ojukwu.*

*Frederick Forsyth, 2003.* Das blaue Sofa, Flickr.

Chukwuemeka Odumegwu Ojukwu, president of secessionist Biafra, was wearing an unbuttoned general's jacket over grubby fatigues. The jacket was in deference to the importance of the occasion. I stood in line with four others and met his eyes for, perhaps, ten seconds. He looked tired and thinner than in photographs.

'You were the one who got my cousin out of the UK,' he said, a statement not a question.[23]

'Yes, sir.'

'You shot down that Mig-17.' This was not a question either.

I nodded.

'Thank you,' he said, pinning a medal to my clean T-shirt, the best I had to wear at short notice, and he moved on down the line.

It was an odd war with strange bedfellows, much forgotten now, mainly with embarrassment by the British. In 1967, Ojukwu declared the eastern region of Nigeria an independent state and a million people died, mostly from starvation. Harold Wilson refused to withdraw support from the Federal Government whatever atrocity it committed, and was aided by the United States and by Russia.

France meanwhile moved in on the Biafran side. The Portuguese, although Britain's oldest ally, turned a blind eye to Biafran support and allowed the use of their airports at Lisbon, Faro and their Atlantic islands, for relief flights of food and medicine and, more quietly, armaments. It was a confusing assembly of European nations disturbed by Britain's inflexibility in the face of starvation caused by its management of the food blockade.

The story of how I found myself flying for the rebel regime is told in another book.[24] I first flew in from São Tomé, an idyllic Atlantic island. There was a grey haze over the airport, the air hot and dripping, smelling like an old wet dog drying in the sun. We were in the Bight of Biafra, the armpit of Africa, the home of slavery, tribal wars, ivory and palm oil, the lubricant for the first steam locomotives and the soapy foundation of the fortunes of the Lever family. A few Irish missionaries from Biafra were busy with relief cargoes while we passengers were corralled in the scruffy, stale and sweaty airport lounge which buzzed with flies as geckos waited patiently on the walls. The drinks machine was broken and the *Coca-Cola* warm and sticky.

The last leg into Biafra was flown at night. The pilot took a long, twisty route which doubled the flight time, but avoided Nigerian fighters and flak. About an hour before landing, the cabin and navigation lights snapped off without warning. I knew there was no radar, no instrument landing system; pilots

---

23 Heal, Chris, *Disappearing,* Chapter 2 (C&S Publishing 2019).
24 *Disappearing,* Chapter 3.

depended on radio beacons, some of them mobile, and a primitive radio. A neat pattern of tiny landing lights appeared below for less than thirty seconds: Uli, part of the road from Owerri to Ihiala, turned into a busy international runway.

Uli was never used during the day. Its disguise was simple, but effective. The widened road verges, loading bays and airport buildings were camouflaged with palm fronds while the main runway was left uncovered. From the air, it was a long, boring stretch of open highway only twenty-one metres compared with a normal runway more than twice as wide. Landing at night was dangerous enough, but it was made worse by the steady, closely-stacked line of aged relief and supply planes that waited out of sight. The skills and experience of their crews were variable. Timing was crucial. A Russian bomber or a converted DC-4 or DC-3, tauntingly broadcasted warnings. When the tell-tale lights came on, it attempted to join the queue of incoming planes, dropping bombs onto the runway and firing at the momentarily highlighted laden freighters. Early most mornings, Russian-supplied MiG jet fighters, flown by Egyptian and British pilots, rocketed and machine-gunned any planes visible on the ground. If fighting was nearby, the Nigerian shells came from British-donated guns and armoured vehicles.

Our plane, a Lockheed Constellation, stayed high, a security precaution. Then, the pilot spiralled tightly downwards as on a helter-skelter funfair ride. We could see lights, palm trees and two church spires flashing past through gusts of rain and blotches of heavy cloud. We gently made contact, hit a badly-filled crater, lurched, lifted a little, and ran smoothly in and pulled sharply off the road into the trees.

All the government rest houses were named Progress Hotel. I unpacked by candlelight: torches, pills to make the poisonous water drinkable, mosquito repellent, gadgets to remove boy scouts from horses' hooves. I left the tins in my bag and inched into an old-fashioned bed with steel sides, a lumpy odorous mattress and sagging springs. The net gave no real protection from mosquitoes or other flying creatures that slipped through its many holes. Bats crawled up the outside. Perspiration saturated my sheets and pillow. The night seemed endless as I listened to the unfamiliar sounds: insects hummed, frogs croaked with gusto, small lizards scuttled, black beetles crackled. After the cicadas, the geckos began, calling to each other from opposite sides of the room. By three, everything had stopped except one small bird with a cry of one pure unwavering note. As the light started to reach the room, there was a sound 'like a silver coin falling against a rock' following by a growling moan. I was told later it was a cobra singing.

I found an ex-pat clubhouse for an afternoon palm wine. There were a dozen desultory drinkers at the club which had seen happier times. The Europeans I talked to seemed to muddle through the daily air strikes, little food, and suspect drinking water, malaria and occasional typhoid. In the corner, a fresh-faced young man was tapping away at a typewriter. I recognised Freddie Forsyth from occasional appearances on the BBC. This was the writer who was was to take the literary and film world by storm with *The Day of the Jackal*.

I plonked my last bottle of whisky on the table and asked him for more information about the war. He talked almost non-stop for the next two hours, a bitter and angry young man. Disgusted by the anti-Biafran bias of the BBC, he resigned just before he was fired and last year returned as a freelance. It was obvious that he was close to Ojukwu, the Biafran leader.[25]

Britain's misguided policy, Forsyth declared, began with a biased and flawed analysis by Sir David Hunt, Britain's High Commissioner in Lagos, for whom Forsyth had few good words. The policy had been adopted by the Commonwealth Relations Office, taken over and intensified by the Foreign Office, and 'cravenly endorsed' by Harold Wilson and Michael Stewart. Hunt's second wife, the dynamic and glamorous Iro Myrianthousis, whose family had large trading interests in West Africa, was a journalist in her own right as editor of the *Lagos Weekly*.

Forsyth wasn't alone in his views. Walter Schwartz in his later book said:

*For years, Whitehall's political thinking on Nigeria had been based on a resolute refusal to face the realities, an obstinate conviction that with enough pulling and shoving the facts could be made to fit the theory, and*

---

25 After the war, Forsyth's anger spilled over, particularly, into three books which I have used liberally to try to recapture our first conversation: *Biafra Story*, 1969; *Emeka*, 1982; and *Outsider*, 2016. He also provided regular assistance to other books on the war like Draper, *Shadows*, 1999, and Venter, *Biafra's War*, 2015. Author de St Jorre noted, decades after that war, that 'you only have to spend a short while with Freddie Forsyth before he lets loose - sometimes vituperatively'. Forsyth took strong issue against the role of the supposedly neutral BBC, especially its external service, which became a powerful pro-Nigerian and anti-Biafran lobbying medium. Editorial comments were liberally infused, he insisted, into what were supposed to be factual news reports.

a determination to brush under the carpet all those manifestations which tend to discredit the dream. It is an attitude which continues to this day.[26]

But why? Forsyth cited a conversation he had with American Consul James Barnard, who explained that the 'single immutable political reality' of Nigeria, was that in any 'race for the material benefits of life, staring from the same point and on the basis of equal opportunity', the easterners [the Igbos, pronounced *ee,bo*] are 'going to win by a mile'. This was intolerable to the North [the Hausa]. The only way to prevent it happening was to impose artificial shackles to progress on the East. This was intolerable to the Easterners. In every sense, claimed Forsyth, Biafra was the most developed country in Africa with more industry, the highest per capita income, the highest purchasing power, the greatest density of roads, schools, hospitals, business houses and factories.

Forsyth moved with enthusiastic distaste to Britain's covert involvement in the war. For twelve months, he said, every possible effort was made by parliament, press and public to ask the Wilson government what was going on. In parliamentary answer after answer, the questioners and the House were 'misled, deceived, rebuffed and frustrated'. Government spokesmen deliberately told the House that the British government was neutral only to admit ten months later that they were not and never had been. In 1968, Wilson told the Commons, arms were supplied exactly on the basis that they had been in the past and that no special provision was made for the needs of the war – despite the growth of the Nigerian army by ten times from 8,000 to 80,000 men. Lorryloads of shells and bullets sped through the night in covered trucks to Gatwick. Arms went to Nigeria out of the British Rhine Army stocks at Antwerp: notably mortars, artillery shells and fresh supplies of Saladin and Ferret armoured cars not only to make up losses, but to expand armoured contingents considerably. The government was even reduced to arguing that if the British didn't supply the weapons then someone else would.

With relish, Forsyth quoted word perfect, for I checked later, a speech in the Lords by The Earl of Cork and Orrery:

*It is the same as saying that if somebody is going to supply the arms in any case, then why not we? But unless you are going to insist that the purpose*

---

26 Schwarz, *Nigeria*, 1968.

> *for which they are going to be used contains no evil – and I do not see how you can say that – then this is an argument that no honourable government can use, for it is the classic self-justification of the black marketeer, the looter, the drug pedlar ... a burst of nine mm bullets in an African stomach is an evil thing any way you reckon it, and if we send those bullets from England knowing that they may so be used, then that particular share in the general evil is ours, and that share is neither diminished nor magnified by a hair's breadth by the likelihood that if we did not send these bullets they would be sent by someone else.*

To add to the British involvement in the blockade, the armoured cars and ammunition, the 'approved' pilots, and the odd mercenary, British NCOs arrived to help with communications. Biafran forces noted a phase of distinct and costly improvement on the front line. And, then, rumours long persisted that part of London's extensive help to Lagos had been the presence of British special forces. 'Political denial has always been a bit too shrill,' announced Forsyth and helped finish the bottle.

'Well, you did ask,' he concluded. 'The main question is how many children will die before it is all over.'

I set about trying to understand more about the famine that filled British newspapers and was, to my mind, why I was there. A stream of refugees trudged through Uli carrying all they had. There was no doubt that the average person was suffering from the rise in prices and shortages imposed by the blockade. Beef had risen from three to sixty shillings a pound, but was seldom obtainable; eggs, once four shillings a dozen were thirty-eight; a chicken at perhaps fifteen shillings before the war rose first to £5, then £15; stockfish, the mainstay of the airlift, had gone from five shillings a pound to sixty; and, most dramatically, salt, once one penny a cup, was now twenty shillings. Rats, snails and mice all fetched a good price. Soap, cosmetics, most items of clothing and, of course, medicines were in short supply. Cigarettes and beer were unobtainable.

Some days later, back in Faro, Portugal, I found three Luftwaffe C-47 Dakotas sitting forgotten on the tarmac alongside some RAF-surplus Meteor jets. Papers said that the DC-3s were sold for $5,000 each; then a middleman called Ernest Koenig paid $11,000 each, while the Biafrans agreed on $45,000 on receipt in Biafra. Two planes were to make the last leg of the transfer with a third kept in Faro in reserve. When I checked my plane over, I realised another irony: it had played a central role in the Berlin Airlift in 1948 and 1949, making dozens of flights for the United States Air Force flying food and medicine into the city to beat the Russian blockade. Later, the plane had been handed over to the West Germans as part of a plan to bolster the new Luftwaffe.

I left Faro at the beginning of April with a sixty-five-year-old American pilot and 6,000 pounds of tinned food, dried stockfish and medicines. In later reports, the co-pilot was believed to be named Grimwood, but, in fact, I was called Grinward. I did almost all the flying as it turned out my captain had limited experience of C-47s, and, as well, he needed his sleep.

We staged around West Africa: the Portuguese island of Porto Santo off Madeira, Bissau, and Abidjan where we were caught in a severe rainstorm. The unpressurised C-47 was built for bad weather, but showed it was true to type with constant leaks around the windshield. I spent an hour wearing an improvised leather apron to try to keep dry and warm. On the final night sector to Uli via São Tomé another standard fault developed when the port oil cooler sprang a leak, the pressure dropped, and I had to shut down the engine.

After a little thought, I placed a telephone call to a engineer friend, called Stan, at Gatwick and asked him how he was doing. He was beyond morose. He jumped at joining me.

At Uli, we needed the whisky he brought when we were told of our mission. It was a madcap idea with little chance of success or survival. We were to convert the two Dakotas into gunships based on the successful adaptation used by the Americans in Vietnam. The big difference was that the fast-firing nine mm guns at the rear and along the inside of the fuselage would fire upwards, not downwards. Our first target was the Nigerian MiG 17F that attacked Uli most dawns. The attack profile of the MiG was almost always the same. The first pass was at altitude before losing height quickly to make a low run across the airstrip from the north. The armed C-47s were to be airborne before first light, making for Uli just above the palm tops, one aircraft from the north and one from the south. Each aircraft was to fly low and to the right of a centre line so as not to be on a collision course. The crew would be advised by a ground controller when the MiG-17 began its run. Then, all of the guns aboard the two C-47s would be fired upwards in such a manner that the Nigerian bomber would literally fly through a shower of bullets.

I took my plane the fifteen miles to Uga, north-east of Uli, an airstrip on the road from Orlu to Awka. The Dakota was pushed back into the bush and camouflaged with leaves and branches and Stan and I set to work on our maintenance and conversion with the help of some bright local trainee engineers. It took two months, mostly while waiting for our guns.

The effects of the blockade were becoming more evident each day. The total shut-off of protein-rich foodstuffs was having its effect. No one had foreseen this because no one had thought the war would last this long.

The priests and nuns knew what they were looking at: kwashiorkor, extreme protein deficiency, which transformed an incompetent bush war into a massive humanitarian tragedy the like of which neither Africa, nor Europe, nor North America had even seen. The children died in the villages, by the roadsides and, alongside those who survived on the relief food, in the feeding centres and, sad to say, there were two near us at Uga. They were built around the local missions, church, school, dispensary and a field the size of a football pitch where the wasted children lay on the grass, on rush mats or the laps of their mothers, who held them close, watching them wither and slip away. As the effects of kwashiorkor intensified, the dark brown curly hair diminished to a ginger frizz. The eyes lost focus, but appeared immense in the wizened face. The weakness of departed muscle made them listless until, unable to move at all, they passed away and a figure in a cassock came to intone a last blessing and take them to the pit.

We spent a few hours each day, digging.

The day of the trap was set for the third of June. Two worn-out thirty-year-old piston-engined military transports were to take on a Russian jet fighter that was the American's primary adversary in Vietnam. In its lower nose, the MiG carried some of the largest guns ever used for air-to-air combat, two twenty-three mm and one thirty-seven mm cannons. It could make 30,000 feet in three minutes, while the Dakota was so old it could just make 20,000. The MiG's top speed was over 700 mph, twice what we could manage after we had warmed up for thirty minutes. The MiG was renowned for its nimbleness; 'steady' might best describe the Dakota. I didn't expect to come back.

We had had three days of practice runs and co-ordination with our partner plane. We both took off twenty minutes before dawn and mooched about out of sight of Uli about fifty feet above the palm tops. We had landmarks which we had to cross at the same time so as to catch the MiG on the line of the road after it came out of its strafing run. The three aircraft had to meet at the same time when we had to fire for three seconds and then the target-hunting MiG would be gone.

Ground control sent the alert. The MiG had been spotted. Then, 'Go, go'. We went. I saw the MiG above and behind the other Dakota. Its pilot appeared more than surprised; no one flew at Uli in the early dawn. He was too close and too high to fire and he pulled his nose to go round again for his easy prey. For that reason, he didn't see me as both C-47s opened up as he flashed over. My plane seemed about to fall apart as Stan let rip and the wall of bullets leapt upwards. It was over almost as it began and I dived left for cover. Stan had a good view and saw the jet soar upwards and, then, a trickle of smoke which became a steady plume. The MiG, still under control, fell out of a stall turn, spotted our sister plane and raked it before heading west back to Nigerian territory.

It was an impulse and stupid, but I banked and followed at a respectful distance. The MiG's speed was well down. Stan joined me and our two Biafran gunners crowded me from behind, whooping as if the war was won. Crossing the Niger river, we were vulnerable, but the smoke from the MiG got thicker, then flames, and the engine cut. The pilot ejected and the MiG came down nose first and exploded in thick bush east of Kwale. It made quite a fire.

Stan noted the position and I turned abruptly and headed for Uli before the sky filled with vengeful Nigerians. We swaggered past the pilot as he dangled downwards. I thought about flying straight into him as a hate burned inside me. Before I could decide, he stuck up two fingers which suggested he might have been British. There was a burst of gunfire from the back of my plane. No one said anything.

The other C-47 had landed safely on one engine, a riddled mid-fuselage, one Igbo gunner with a flesh wound in the arm. The aircraft was irreparable and was run deep into the bush. The pilot had seen nothing and reported the mission a failure. The assumption was that we had been shot down and that explains why, instead of a hero's welcome, the Biafran anti-aircraft fire welcomed us as we approached. We were too low to be inconvenienced, but the black flak clouds attracted a MiG. I made it down and lost no time in turning into cover, but the manoeuvre was slow enough for the jet to see where I had gone. The four of us ran deep into the palms and dived into the insects and rotting foliage as the MiG ripped open our valiant plane. The smoke guided the pilot back for a second go. When all was clear, Stan was near tears as he realised that not even he would ever fix that pile of wreckage.

That's how I got my medal and met President Ojukwu.

# IAN RICHARD KYLE PAISLEY

## Baron Bannside, Protestant religious leader, Northern Ireland

If there was one man who towered over political and religious life of all sects and all opinions in Northern Ireland it was Ian Paisley. He became a Protestant evangelical minister in 1946, the year before I was born, founded and led the Democratic Unionist Party (DUP) from 1971 to 2008 and was the Northern Irish first minister for over a year towards the end of his career.

Paisley either galvanised or frightened people as a hardline and outspoken firebrand fighting for continued union with England, the true definition of human *Marmite*. He seized every opportunity and welcomed any pulpit to deliver his messages: implacably against any involvement by the Republic of Ireland in Northern Irish affairs, and thus

*Ian Paisley, 1994.* European Union.

against any form of compromise: anti-Catholic, anti-ecumenic and a stalwart against homosexuality. Paisley promulgated a highly conservative form of Biblical literalism and had no truck with opposing or nuanced views.

In 1971, I spent two weeks with the 2nd Parachute Regiment of the British Army, based just outside Belfast. The city was relatively quiet after the riots of three years before. Groups of soldiers were often given permission to go into bars and entertainment centres away from the no-go areas. Paisley had recently been released early from prison as part of a general amnesty, sentenced for unlawful assembly which led to vicious riots. Paisley's men, armed with nail-studded cudgels, took over Belfast centre to prevent a march by Catholic and civil rights groups. Later, the Ulster Protestant Volunteers (UPV) bombed water and electricity installations in the North leaving much of Belfast without power and water. The UPV was the paramilitary wing of the Ulster Constitution Defence Committee (UCDC), also founded by Paisley. Paisley had recently won the North Antrim seat in the UK general election and was on the verge of forming the DUP.

Word spread through the officers of the Para, that Paisley was to give a sermon at the Martyrs Memorial Free Presbyterian church in Belfast's Ravenhill Road. The Church, of which he was the moderator, demanded strict segregation from 'any church which has departed from the fundamental doctrines of the Word of God'. A group of three young lieutenants decided, in a genuine spirit of enquiry I felt, to go along and hear at first hand what the man had to say. Despite all the violence and angry rhetoric, the troops were actually on the same side, were they not, fighting to maintain Northern Ireland's place as a part of the United Kingdom?

I asked to join the party and was accepted.

We found seats in a middle pew of a crowded church. Another five minutes and we would have been standing at the back or in the overflow that reached onto the pavement and some distance along the main road. We were dressed in civvies, no evidence of uniforms, but our ages, youthful faces and short hair gave us away. There was a buzz, everyone knew everyone. Calls were made from row to row with a lot of dark sectarian humour. However, what we four quickly realised was that we were not part of the congregation, not part of the community and not well loved.

Of course, as young men, we knew how to appear cool, how to weather the emotional disconnect. We chatted among ourselves, pointed to unusual items, gazed intelligently about with interested expressions.

But, we knew how uncomfortable we really felt. And everyone else knew it, too. We were foreigners, by upbringing, by race, by religion and by politics. We were not trusted or welcome.

The meeting began with prayers and readings. Biblical extracts hardly needed to be said out loud as they were mouthed confidently and silently in support. There was no conventional service and certainly no hint of papist ceremonial or ritual. It was a religious and political performance, a statement of defiance and solidarity, of rejection and of belief.

Paisley, a big man, climbed the steps and grasped the lectern. His strongly-accented voice was amplified by powerful speakers throughout the building. No one in the crowd, inside or out, could fail to hear him and to wilt under his fervour. His combed back, greased hair flopped forward with the effort. He was captivating and frightening at the same time. His conviction rolled over his audience and seized them by the heart and head. He was a born leader. His personality dominated. To doubt his message was to doubt oneself. Such self belief must come from true righteousness.

I can remember little today of his actual content, but every statement was backed by quotations from the Bible, a copy of which he often waved in confirmation. His distaste for the Roman church flew everywhere alongside his spittle. Catholics were led by the Antichrist. In parts, it seems that every sentence was sprinkled with the name of murdered Protestants.

When Princess Maragaret and the Queen Mother met Pope John XXIII in 1958, he recalled, he denounced them for 'committing spiritual fornication and adultery' by associating with the man. When John died five years later, Paisley told his audience that 'this Romish man of sin is now in Hell'.

One could smell the hatred in the church, the rise of body hormones and the sense the willingness for terrible action.

With a final dramatic denunciation and call for solidarity, he was done, standing alone in God's pulpit, arms limp by his side, head bowed, eyes still flashing under bushy brows. There was a period of silence, almost of shock, then the hall burst into a steady, ominous thunder of clapping hands and stamping feet with occasional yells.

Had that been the end of it, the event may not have qualified for one of my 'personal moments' as, despite the tidal wave, there had been no element of individual contact. I was one of the crowd, no different from an audience in a theatre or concert.

But it was not the end.

'I ask you to give generously for God's work against popery and the Antichrist,' he said.

There was no conventional collection platter as in a sedate half-empty Church of England morning service. Powerful men arrived at the end of each row and large buckets were passed along. People gave generously, notes and coins, from pre-prepared contributions. As our bucket arrived, we sent it quietly on its way with small coins from our pockets The bucket reached the other end of our row and then retraced its journey and arrived back with us. Confused, we sent it on to where it began.

And back it came.

Paisley's voice filled the hall.

'I see we have within our number,' he said, 'four members of the occupying English armed forces. We can all see you.'

Here, everyone turned around to face us.

'You are here in our country to keep us safe from the atrocities of the IRA. The same IRA that murders our wives and children with bullets and bombs and seeks to undermine our government. It takes money to fight this evil and we expect everyone here who stands with us to contribute generously.'

His eyes bore into us and around us. The hairs prickled on my neck.

The bucket came back for a third time. I was the first to receive it.

I fished out a five pound note, a large sum in those days from a small wage. I made sure that the denomination could be seen. My colleagues followed my lead.

'We thank the British Army for its service,' said Paisley, as the bucket finally went on its way.

## ALAN PETER PASCOE

British Olympic Games hurdler and businessman

## DAME DARCEY ANDREA BUSSELL

English ballerina

## SIR MARTIN STUART SORRELL

British businessman; founder of WPP advertising

*Alan Pascoe.* Chris Smith, Popperfoto.   *Darcey Bussell, 2016.* Theatre Tickets Direct.   *Martin Sorrell, 2022.*

There was a chink, an opportunity. My employer, IBM in the United Kingdom, was looking for innovative ways to shed staff, people whose skills could be easily and more cheaply bought from outside the business than if they remained inside. Already, IBM had hived off a printer arm and the workers who maintained their building infrastructure, facilities management to those in the trade.

Could the powers be persuaded that my team of some thirty people, who provided marketing communications, advertising, promotional literature, mailing, exhibitions and events, sponsorship and the like, might fall into this category?

The trick was to find the initial funding to make the sums add up. Future owners from within the ranks could buy shares in the new business from their redundancy payments in a classic Management Buyout (MBO), but that would not be enough. I had to go to the marketing industry to find additional investors. These companies would have to feel that they had privileged access to bids for IBM's accounts, but also feel the new company would have the wherewithal to make an unusual offering in a crowded marketplace. The difference would be that the business would offer consultants and project managers proven to be capable of assembling and running across-the-board marketing packages. The industry at that time in the early 1990s was built on specialist organisations who saw their own skill, say advertising, as pre-eminent, and the main and often only way to carry a message to market. They didn't do sharing or a balanced approach.

Additionally, I had to persuade IBM of the idea's integrity. This was a problem because IBM at heart, and on its edges, was a sales business. Genuine marketing confused it and that meant irritation at the large sums of money involved for benefits that were not well measured and, frankly, the perceived flakiness in a regimented organisation of some of the protagonists. Overlaying this was a belief by me that IBM was not good at negotiating; that is to say, the company was so big and sure of itself that it could act like an insensitive steamroller. I needed some serious backup to provide managerial backbone and to cover my admitted naivety. We were talking about a multi-million pound deal here.

My solution was a collaboration of some of the top marketing companies in the UK, already IBM suppliers, who would buy preference shares and, thereby, provide the necessary startup cash, but leave the day-to-day management to the new owners. Such an arrangement, not often used, is called a BIMBO (Buy-In Management Buyout).

One of, perhaps, a dozen marketing companies I turned to was Alan Pascoe Associates (later API). Pascoe was from Portsmouth, IBM's UK home, and a university educated ex-teacher. He made his name in the hurdles and relays at three successive Olympic Games, the European Athletic Championships, and the Commonwealth and European Indoor Games. After, he finished competing, Pascoe became involved in events marketing and consulting and built a successful business.

I arranged to meet him late one winter morning at his London headquarters. I took with me one of my employees-to-be who had the lead on sponsorship. He was nervous about the deal with Pascoe, his own strength was in the arts and he did not want to be subsumed in a wholly commercial organisation oblivious to the delicacies of concerts, festivals, performing egos and the like. We agreed that he would excuse himself if the meeting got personal.

On the train, we got two phone calls (the early mobiles were like concrete bricks), one after the other. The first, from Pascoe's secretary, said there was a mini in-house crisis and could we delay the meeting for an hour? Alan would be in our debt.

Peter's phone rang. His contacts in the arts world, many of which had become friends due to his discretion, were legendary. The call was from Darcey Bussell, perhaps the most prestigious English ballerina of her era.

She had a problem. 'Could Peter spare her thirty minutes?'

I went along as supplementary baggage. We sat in the window of a coffee shop in Covent Garden near to her working home at The Royal Ballet, where, at twenty, she became the youngest ever principal dancer.

She was delightful and stunning, even in her off-duty jeans. I was in awe. I tried to separate myself slightly as the two had a heartfelt and intimate conversation. It was obvious that she trusted my colleague absolutely. After some minutes of enquiry into the state of her feet, a subject never to be taken lightly in discussion with a dancer, the problem surfaced. Suffice to say, it concerned a full-length portrait of her by the artist Allen Jones which had been commissioned by London's National Portrait Gallery.

Difficulty resolved, we met Alan Pascoe who was charming, very fit and full of apologies, but the meeting was hopeless. Pascoe could see no advantage to his business in joining with ours. What he wanted was full access and control of Darcey Bussell's friend, but balked at the money I was paying. At an agreed sign, my colleague slipped from the room giving me meaningful looks. The meeting quicky broke down in good humour and we left.

A few years later, Pascoe sold API to a large conglomerate. I suspect my colleague was right; he would have been subsumed.

However, a satisfactory combination of investors was assembled and I pitched to a stand-in board of IBM and got approval for the new company. We had a good couple of years until the roof fell in entirely outside of our influence. IBM in the USA decided to centralise all its world-wide advertising with one agency. Our business model was broken. The UK subsidiary was instructed to break its contract with us. IBM still remained eighty per cent of our turnover as we had not had long to diversify. Heavy redundancies and even closure loomed large.

There followed long and hard negotiations over compensation.

One of the options was in our hands and that was to sell the business as a broken reed. The advertising agency chosen by IBM was owned by WPP, the world's largest advertising and public relations group. WPP had been founded by Martin Sorrell, descended of Jewish immigrants, who had studied economics at Christ's College, Cambridge, and gained an MBA from Harvard University. We made an approach and were checked out at our Basingstoke offices. Passed fit to talk to, I travelled to London with an almost empty knapsack. I was looking to save jobs.

What can one say about Martin Sorrell? He was a self-made man who began from almost nothing and perfected the art of the 'earn out', hugely successful, very rich and used to getting his own way. He stunned the advertising world in 1987 with a $566 million hostile takeover of J. Walter Thompson. He followed this in 1989 with another dramatic hostile $825 million purchase of Ogilvy and Mather. Group Chairman David Ogilvy publicly referred to Sorrell as an 'odious little shit'. I felt as I went into my meeting that I was already on a greasy slope despite the excellent coffee.

The difficulty was that Sorrell didn't get the concept of a one-shop, all services marketing project management business. He was steeped in his dozens of individual agencies, all competing one with another. We argued back and forwards, up and down, and I got nowhere. There came a time when I just stood up, offered him my hand and thanked him for his time.

As I left reception, my intermediary said, 'No one has ever done that to him before, deciding to leave. He normally just peremptorily dismisses people after he's worn them down. He'll remember you.'

The irony was that about five years later, I read in a newspaper that Sorrell had just launched a new type of agency which offered cross-skill project management to large businesses.

There you go. Ahead of time again.

# COLIN TREVOR PILLINGER

## English planetary scientist; Beagle 2 Mars lander

Professor Colin Pillinger was pronounced a failure by those quick to judge when he 'lost' *Beagle 2*, a Mars lander and European Space Agency (ESA) project.[27] After the spacecraft failed to check in, the commission and their director of science pinned some of the blame on Pillinger's management. In turn, Pillinger cited lack of support from key figures at ESA.

Twelve years later, *Beagle 2* was found by NASA to have successfully touched down in the expected landing area of *Isidis Planita*, an impact basin near to the Mars equator. One of its four solar panels had failed to open, the failed panel blocking its transmitter.

*Colin Pillinger, 2009.* Mike Peel, University of Manchester.

Pillinger was a man of many parts. He enlisted the British rock band, *Blur*, to write a song intended to be Beagle 2's call sign when it began work. He also persuaded artist Damien Hirst to provide a spot painting to use in calibrating the spacecraft's camera.

Colin Pillinger was an English planetary scientist and a founding member of the Planetary and Space Sciences Research Institute in Milton Keynes. He held numerous university positions and was a Fellow of the Royal Astronomical,

---

27 Pillinger, Colin, *Beagle – from Sailing Ship to Mars Spacecraft* (2003).

Geographical and Meteoritical Societies. He may have been just as proud to be a patron of the Shrewsbury International Cartoon Festival, a trustee of the National Maritime Museum, and in holding honorary memberships of the *Blur* Fan Club and the *Eagle* Comic Society.

I first met Colin's sister, Doreen Lindegaard, while I was studying for a PhD into the felt hatting industry at Bristol University. My research covered many of the villages around Bristol, especially in South Gloucestershire. The family came from nearby Kingswood. Doreen was an enthusiastic supporter, often opening avenues on her well-respected and copious website, *Bristol Family History*, and through her own research.[28] She even asked for and received a guided tour of some of the village manufactories.

One day, I shared with her one of my research problems. I had found that among the papers at the Royal Society was a copy of a little known study by Robert Hooke written in 1666 into how to improve techniques in the felt trade. Hooke sought unsuccessfully to stir interest among fellow Society members whom he felt should do more to use their skills in the everyday world. I heard that, as part of his lecture, attended by Samuel Pepys, Hooke shared a drawing of the felt hatmaking process, evidently already well established. This drawing and its description would prove invaluable to me in my thesis.

In those days, the Royal Society was an invitation fellowship of many of the world's most eminent scientists. It remains the oldest scientific academy in continuous existence.

It was also less accessible than it is today. My requests for research access were turned down with an almost audible, 'Tut. Tut.' I was only a PhD student.

Robert Hooke became one of the most important scientists of his time – called England's Leonardo. He was a polymath, active as a physicist, astronomer, geologist, meteorologist and architect – as well as seeking out improvements to the industries of his day. He was credited as one of the first to investigate living things at microscopic level using a compound microscope that he designed. After the Great Fire of London, he performed more than half of the property surveys necessary for the city's rapid rebuild. As a student, he built the vacuum pumps used by Robert Boyle for his gas law. In 1664, he identified the rotations of Mars and Jupiter. He inferred a wave theory of light. He also suggested that gravity obeys an inverse square law and applied it to planetary

---

28 bristolfamilyhistoryblog.wordpress.com/author/dplindegaard.

motion, a principle furthered by Isaac Newton (which contributed to great rivalry between the two men). He also argued that mountains were elevated by geological processes and presaged the theory of biological evolution.

It was Doreen who suggested that her younger brother, elected a fellow of the Royal Society in 1993, might be able to help me. We had a lengthy phone conversation in which I was quizzed in a humorous but determined way about my subject. I passed that test and he suggested we meet at his dairy farm. I found him in his wheelchair, a victim of progressive multiple sclerosis which prevented him from doing physical work.

He was full of warm welcomes and genuine interest. He was surrounded by his dogs. He told me that the greatest pleasure now in his life was to come home, open the door and be slobbered over by his canine friends.

With good cheer, I passed this test also.

The welcome at the Royal Society in Carlton House Terrace, a grand white stucco-faced house on the street's south side, which overlooked The Mall and St James's Park, was reverential. My sponsor was a legend. The required papers were laid out ready, my registration card already mostly filled in.

Hooke's drawings, script and annotated corrections were invaluable for my work. Discovering such finds can be ecstatic for the dedicated researcher. The detail, spread over many pages, put several academic myths on the origins of the trade and its practices to the sword.

Thank you to Doreen and to Colin, who died in Cambridge after a brain haemorrhage in 2014.

# MIKE JOHN PROCTOR AND CLIVE EDWARD BUTLER RICE

## South African cricket allrounders

*Mike Proctor, 1981.*     *Clive Rice, 1982.*

Half an hour earlier, the thunder clouds opened and the rain raced to earth. Forked lightning stabbed across the sky. Even the hardiest souls dashed for cover while being careful not to stand near metal posts.

Just as quickly, the skies cleared and burning sunshine brought spurts of vapour from sodden benches and sports equipment. This was the Wanderers Cricket Stadium in Johannesburg on a Saturday in March 1982. It was the morning of the second day of the first unofficial international 'Test' between South Africa and the South African Breweries English XI, a sub-par and under-prepared side, but which did claim some genuine ageing stars like Denis Amiss, Geoffrey Boycott, John Emburey, Graham Gooch and Alan Knott.

The English team was the first of what would be nine tours by rebel cricketers from around the world (specifically from England, Australia, Sri Lanka and the

West Indies) attracted by a combination of South African rands and, in some cases, dissatisfaction with their home country authorities. Arrangements for this first tour were made in secret and not disclosed until the initial twelve English players climbed down from the plane in Johannesburg for a one-month visit.

South Africa had a policy of choosing international athletes by skin colour. In 1971, an international sports boycott was introduced to 'voice global disapproval of these selection policies and of apartheid in general'. South Africa became a sporting outcast. As well as Test Cricket, they were banned from the Olympics, the FIFA World Cup and international rugby union.

The English players expected a brief public outcry and a slap on the wrist from the ICC, the International Cricket Council. They could not have been more wrong. The team was subject to global outrage, particularly among the UK Press and politicians. In parliament, they were dubbed the 'dirty dozen'. The rebels, who numbered fifteen after hiring three more players to cover injuries, all received three-year bans from international cricket and the suspensions ended the careers of more than half the squad, including Boycott, then the world's leading Test run scorer.

I regained my glistening wooden bench seat, dug out my waterproof cushion, and heard the announcer call that lunch would be taken early. Play might start again in an hour's time because of the efficiency of the new pitch's drainage system. Like almost every other spectator, I had my cool bag of Castle beers, a plentiful supply of biltong and some pork pies. I noticed numbers of the players of both teams spreading though the crowd in a display of goodwill and thanks for attending.

Then, a chunky gentleman in whites slumped onto the bench beside me.

'Spare a beer?'

It was Mike Proctor, the South African, the same age as me and, in my certain opinion, one of the greatest allrounders ever to play the game.

'Of course, Mr Proctor, Sir.' I reached into my bag, cracked a can and offered it to him.

'Not allowed to drink, you know.' He paused and took a long swallow. 'At least while the game's on.' He passed his can to me so I had one can in each hand. 'Bloody tele cameras. Always catch you out. What's your name?"

'Chris. Biltong?' He took a fulsome handful.

'Happy with the way the game's going? Everyone's contributing.'

South Africa had opened the batting the day before and had nearly three hundred runs with only two wickets down. Barry Richards had hit, for him, a slow sixty-six; Jimmy Cook, a carefully authoritative one hundred and fourteen. Peter Kirsten and Graeme Pollock were at the wicket with already a century stand. Richards, Cook, Kirsten and Pollock, four of the greatest batsmen of any era from any team. Proctor, in next after Clive Rice, was perhaps the outstanding batter of his generation. He was one of only three players to score six consecutive centuries in first class cricket, alongside Don Bradman and C B Fry.

'Yeah, mate, it's going well. Just hope my knee holds up when we get to bowl.'

He took another pull from the can I was guarding. Proctor had just retired from leading Gloucestershire in English county cricket, renamed Proctorshire by many, in honour of his over twenty thousand runs and more than one thousand wickets. He was a phenomenon.

'Hey, Ricey,' he yelled suddenly. 'Chris, here's got a spare cold one.'

Wandering down through the stands was captain Clive Rice. If Mike Proctor was the leading South African all-rounder of all time, Rice was not far behind. He was talked of in the same breath as Imran Khan, Ian Botham, Kapil Dev and Richard Hadlee. His international career was also blighted by apartheid and the bans on the national side. He was in the middle of his captaincy of Nottinghamshire County Cricket Club.

'Thanks, mate,' he said and sat the other side of me. I was left holding three cans. 'I wonder what the rain will do to the wicket?'

The bell sounded on cue from the clubhouse signifying the game would start in ten minutes.

'Need to get my pads on,' said Rice, 'although there's a good chance I won't be needed. You needn't bother Prock as you're next in after me.'

They both took a last surreptitious chug covered by raised elbows and sauntered back to the changing room. Proctor also took another handful of biltong.

'Thanks, mate,' they chimed.

Rice couldn't have been more wrong. Kirsten was out almost immediately on resumption and Rice seemed a little unsure of himself as he strode to the wicket. He scratched around for a few balls then was out for one, caught behind by Alan Knott. Proctor faired no better, also out for one and caught by Knott.

It may have been my fancy, but I thought they both looked ruefully in my direction as they left the field.

Had my hospitality single-handedly altered the course of the match? I needn't have worried. Graeme Pollock saw his side through to a declaration at four hundred, Vince van der Bijl took five wickets and South Africa enforced the follow on. After a couple of early scares, South Africa quickly knocked off the required thirty-seven runs. Proctor and Rice didn't bowl or bat again in the match.

I never met either of the men again although I did see them play and did follow their careers a little more closely than before.

Clive Rice was found to have a brain tumour in 1998. In 2015, he collapsed at his home in Johannesburg. Scans showed that his tumour was too deep to be removed by surgery. Rice went to India where the tumour was successfully removed by radiation. A few days later, back in Johannesburg, he died from sepsis, aged sixty-six.

Mike Proctor had a cardiac arrest last year, in 2024. He was admitted to intensive care in Umhlanga, a coastal town north of Durban where he died through complications during routine heart surgery, aged seventy-seven.

# MAJOR THE REVEREND W DAVID RATHS

## Canadian canon of the Cathedral of the Most Holy Trinity, Bermuda

Major and chaplain in the Canadian armed forces ministering to soldiers in war-torn parts of the world, a canon at the Cathedral of the Most Holy Trinity in Bermuda, an annual *habitué* of Glyndebourne and a fellow traveller on a week's tour of the architecture of East Germany's small towns followed by another week of solid Bach, well, you'd expect a bit of decorum.

*David Raths.*

Sedateness isn't Major The Reverend David Raths natural style. He's more of a disrupter, really. I think that's why we got on so well on the coach tour. Wrong questions, wrong humour, wrong voice level, wrong timing, the delight of some, but a worry for the more serious and that included the German lecturer and intensely dedicated and caring tour guide, Dr Karl Kremeier.

By the last day, to the relief of many, David and I sat alone in the coach in the naughty boy seats drinking beer rather than traipse around yet another château.

'Schlossed out,' was the expression.

But, of course, there was a serious side to the conversation. How could there not be? A few evenings before, David confided to me over dinner that he had a plan for a free afternoon on the next day. He had realised that our hotel was near the main Auschwitz Concentration camp. He had never been to one of these camps and he felt it his duty as a soldier and a priest to visit.

Would I go with him? I refused outright. The idea filled me with horror. I had no wish to carry the images that I knew I would see around with me for the rest of my days. David tried a little harder, but soon knew that he would be on his own.

The following day, I sat in the hotel garden with a bottle of brandy waiting for him to return. My guess was that, while we had only recently met, I knew enough of him to be sure that he would be devastated.

Dinner time passed and I got a few sandwiches. David was over an hour later than the expected time. When he did finally turn the corner, he was more slouched than normal, older, walking slowly and obviously deeply affected. He sat at the table, looked at the brandy glass for a while, then swallowed it straight down. He said nothing. I refilled his glass.

Around ten o'clock, I told him the bottle was finished, but I had another in my room. I would get it. There was now a chill in the air. Other tour guests had wandered up, but all immediately sensed that something was badly wrong and left with hardly a word.

Eventually, David gave a sigh that seemed to rise from beneath his feet.

'Chris,' he said slowly, pausing after each word, 'despite all I already knew, I never, never, never thought it would be so awful. I am in real danger of losing my faith. My head is full of a relay of terrible pictures and I can't stop them. You were absolutely right not to go.'

Tears ran down his cheeks.

He didn't say much more. About two in the morning, only kept warm by the brandy, he suggested we went to our rooms.

Auschwitz was a complex of over forty concentration and extermination camps. Above the main gate was the legend, *Arbeit macht frei*, 'work sets you free', and which received the hosts of people crammed into freight trains from all over Europe. The camps were a major part of the Nazis' 'Final Solution to the Jewish question'. Inside the gates, of the 1.3 million people sent there, 1.1 million were murdered, mostly by a very efficient gassing system. The numbers included 960,000 Jews (of whom 865,000 were gassed on arrival), 74,000 non-Jewish Poles, 21,000 Romani, 15,000 Soviet prisoners of war and up to 15,000 others. Those not gassed were murdered by starvation, exhaustion, disease, execution, beatings and by medical experiments.

Later, David stayed at my home in Hampshire a couple of times, near enough to drive to Glyndebourne. Sharing dinner with family, we often discussed out East German trip. We never, never mentioned Auschwitz.

# JON SILKIN

## British poet; founder of Stand magazine

'Clip.' 'Clip.' 'Clop.' 'Clip, clip.' Expletive. 'Can't find it.' Expletive

It was nearly ten o'clock at night and getting dark. There was an early frost waiting behind the crisp hedges. I wore a flat cap and scarf over my pullover.

'Clip, clip.' 'Clop.'

'My game,' shouted my much older opponent and he did a little gig so that his full white beard moved in the moonlight. 'One more,' I think, 'to put you completely in your place, young man.'

We were playing tables tennis in a covered, but open, shelter at the side of a country house in Chalfont St Giles in Buckinghamshire. Facing me was Jon Silkin, 'one of the most distinctive and distinguished of the British poets who began to publish in the 1950s'.

*Jon Silkin, 1975.* Jake Bernard, Flickr.

Around us, couples stared in amazement at the contrast. They had just paid to hear an enthralling and knowledgeable lecture, *The War Poetry of Wilfred Owen and Isaac Rosenberg*, both killed in France in 1918, by the world expert in this field. Fifteen minutes before, many of the members of his audience had been moved to tears by his quotations and their delivery. He included a few of his own poems, like *Death of a Son*, who died in a mental hospital, aged one.

*… He turned over on his side with his one year*
*Red as a wound*

*He turned over as if he could be sorry for this*
*And out of his eyes two great tears rolled, like stones, and he died.*[29]

'(Silkin) was a wonderfully acute, incisive and creatively illuminating critic of others' writing; a most gifted teacher of literature and creative writing to both young and adult students; and at his best a spellbinding reader of his own verse. To observe a large group of cynical and sharp-witted sixth formers, not at all fooled by his pretence that he was working-class, become mesmerised by the quality of his reading, and of what he was reading, was to witness a repeated miracle.'[30]

Now, Jon Silkin was whooping like a teenager with a bat in hand as snow flakes began to tumble.

I was there as a taxi driver and bed provider at my brother's request. Silkin had taken the reading, but had nowhere to stay, money being at a premium. My brother lived at Silkin's house in Jesmond near Newcastle upon Tyne while studying English at the university and worked for him part-time as a van driver taking over his role street selling Silkin's magazine, *Stand*. He often slept in the van. Hence, I was pressed into service and Silkin passed a night in my home in Chalfont St Peter after lowering with me a post table tennis bottle of malt whisky.

Silkin was born in London in 1930 in a Litvak Jewish family. His grandparents were from the Lithuanian part of the Russian Empire. His uncle was Lewis Silkin, a labour politician and later baron, who was Minister for Town, and Country Planning in the Clement Atlee government from 1945. He also founded a famous law firm.

For a time in the fifties, after National Service, Jon Silkin supported himself by manual labour and other menial jobs.

In 1952, Silkin founded *Stand* magazine and kept it running, almost continuously, until his death in 1997. He used his £5 redundancy money, received after trying to organise fellow janitors to fight back against management, to found a publication which would 'stand' against injustice and oppression and 'stand' for the 'role that the arts, poetry and fiction in particular could and should play in that fight'. The first issue had twenty pages of mimeographed

---

29 Silkin, Jon, *The Peaceable Kingdom* (Chatto and Windus, 1954).
30 Pybus, Rodney, 'Obituary', *The Independent* (1/12/1997).

green paper and sold for eight pennies. It was soon a major international vehicle for new poetry and short fiction.

Through *Stand*, Silkin played a midwife's role, at least in part, to many writers who later became prominent, from the playwrights Harold Pinter and David Mercer to poets like Geoffrey Hill, Tony Harrison, Ken Smith, Michael Hamburger, Roy Fisher, Sorley Maclean and Iain Crichton Smith and, later, novelist Peter Carey.

Silkin's obituary noted that the 'stocky, bustling figure of a diminutive Old Testament prophet with white hair and a beard, dressed in clothes left behind from *Waiting for Godot*, has been seen less often badgering queues in the wind and the rain outside cinemas and theatres to buy copies of *Stand*; it was once one of the most familiar sights four times a year in university towns and London'.[31]

It was, I think, the next year that my wife and I decided to holiday for a week in the Newcastle area. Silkin was able to return the favour and we stayed with my brother at Silkin's house. Neither he, nor his wife, the American fiction writer, Lorna Tracy, whom I never met, was at home. There were strict orders to stay out of the library and study.

These clear instructions touched on the other side of Silkin's character which I had first sensed at my home and which others later confirmed.

For a man of potent intellect, he could be 'touchingly naïve and ignorant about the world beyond literary affairs'. His friends described him as 'famously difficult' and who could be 'combative, prickly and vexatious'. But he was 'engagingly funny, a sympathetic and solicitous friend, and endlessly generous with his time'.

I worried reading this short chapter back later, that I have paid nowhere near enough attention to Jon Silkin's books and poetry which is what, for me, marks him out. While at his home, I spent many of the spare hours reading his work (being careful not to enter the library).

He was a leading authority on the poets of the First World War, for instance in his best-known critical work *Out of Battle* (1972). He had an intuitive understanding of the authors' often raw work. Silkin also produced several anthologies of verse, some drawn from *Stand*, like *Poetry of the Committed Individual* (1973). I count forty-eight completed works.

---

31 Pybus, 'Obituary'.

His own work stands every comparison with his own heroes. Try *The Two Freedoms* (1958), *The Re-Ordering of the Stones* (1961), *The Lens-Breakers* (1992) and *Watersmeet* (1994).

Many of these works offer what may be Silkin's major theme, the division between nature and mankind, 'our fall from that paradisal state where the wolf shall dwell with the lamb', images of which one of Silkin's favourite artists, the American Edward Hicks, painted over and over again. Silkin's own collection in 1965, which won the Geoffrey Faber Memorial Prize, was called *Nature with Man* and was an attempt to heal that rift.

## GUY SLATER
English writer, theatre and TV director

## PETER DUNCAN
Blue Peter presenter and Charlie Chaplin in *Little Tramp*, the musical

## LORD RICHARD SAMUEL 'DICKIE' ATTENBOROUGH
English actor, film director and producer

## BRIAN BLESSED
English actor

## SIR CAMERON ANTHONY MACKINTOSH
British theatrical producer and theatre owner

For five years around 1990, I was chairman of the Haymarket Theatre, an unusual combination of part-time repertory company, the Horseshoe, and a 420-seat auditorium which was home for a large number of Basingstoke's amateur musical and theatre organisations. It was owned by the borough council who were wringing their hands trying to staunch a constant drain on the public finances. The theatre's organisation was cumbersome and the business was failing despite loyal and enthusiastic audiences.

*Guy Slater.*

*Peter Duncan, 2006. Flickr.*

*Richard Attenborough, 2007. Flickr.*

Council officers approached my boss, the senior director at IBM locally, for help in sorting things out. I agreed to take a look at the problem. At my first board meeting, I counted thirty-seven individuals, each representing an organisation with a vested interest in a piece of the theatre and all, at least in part, in conflict with one or several other groups.

I said I would take the job only if the whole board resigned. To my surprise, they did. I appointed a new board with seven members, some with business and financial experience from outside the theatrical world. We set about understanding what went on and, for a start, trying to balance the books.

There was, of course, tension between the professional and amateur arms, with little linkage between revenue and the cost of production. The idea of set budgets for each show was widely ignored. Theatrical standards came first, and second, and, if no one was looking, third.

After a lot of heartache all round and a couple of years' work, matters were seen by the owners to be on such an even keel that they agreed to a multi-million pound refurbishment in 1992. The work was detailed: the interior was modernised with a new steel and concrete horseshoe shaped auditorium and included an enlarged stage, a new circle, better ventilation, two new bars, a restaurant and a computerised box office.

Of great personal help to me during the period was Guy Slater who is my first famous name for this chapter. Guy founded the original Horseshoe Theatre Company in 1973/4. Among the stars who appeared in the early days were Peter Cushing, Michael Ball, Timothy West, Derek Jacobi, Richard Murdoch and Prunella Scales (who was also for a short time on the Board).

Guy and I had many long discussions which gave me the confidence to push forward. His CV is too long to list but involves leadership work at theatres in Oxford, Leatherhead, Farnham, Regent's Park (London), the Orange Tree (Richmond), Norwich, Newbury and in California and several others. He has written over thirty TV and radio dramas and stage plays, and directed on TV *Nanny* (three series with Wendy Craig), *Miss Marple* (three series with Joan Hickson) and *Love Hurts* (three series with Adam Faith and Zoë Wanamaker). Among his five books is the excellent *Hurricane Maggie*, based in part of his time in Havana, Cuba, where his father was British Ambassador. One wishes he had written more.

*Brian Blessed, 2012.* Calum Gilchrist, Flickr.

When not talking about theatre, Guy and I spent our time discussing affairs in Myanmar (Burma) for which he had great affection and deplored the repressive situation.

One of the sadder aspects of my chairmanship was the decision to release the long-time artistic director, Ian Mullins. Ian was a gentle and kind man, steeped in regional theatres. In the sixties, he probably saved the Everyman Theatre in Cheltenham and then became director of the repertory companies in Salisbury and Farnham, before moving to Basingstoke, and also to the Mercury Theatre in Auckland, New Zealand.

*Cameron Mackintosh, 2022.* Edwardx.

Ian retired to Christchurch, New Zealand, to be near his two sons and their families and worked as a freelance director and actor. Ian died there in 2014, aged eighty-five.

Ian's replacement was Adrian Reynolds who worked in Chelmsford and in Ontario, Canada, before moving to the Byre Theatre at St Andrews where he spent a very successful ten years. Tragedy struck after I left the board (I thought five years was sufficient) when Adrian died suddenly of a major heart attack in 1998, aged fifty-six.

It was to Adrian that I entrusted the first production to reopen the Haymarket in 1992/3 after its refurbishment. He excelled himself by identifying and chasing down the world premiere of *Little Tramp*, a musical of the life of Charlie Chaplain. The leading role was taken by Peter Duncan, supported by among others John Altman from the original cast of the BBC soap opera, *Eastenders*. I never met Altman other than in passing, but I had several chats with Duncan and he is my second famous name.

Duncan was presenter of *Blue Peter* in the 1980s, made a series of travel documentaries and appeared in a host of stage and TV productions. He founded the *National Adventure*, a company specialising in self-guided walking and cycling holidays which operates in fifty-eight countries. He also found time to become Chief Scout. He was good fun to talk to and was a fund of information and contacts. He could sing, too.

Theatrical royalty visited *Little Tramp* at the Haymarket. Dickie Attenborough arrived in a large car and greeted all and sundry with a wave of his right hand. I had a handshake as board chairman and a greeting. Staff swooned at the presence. Bushy-bearded Brian Blessed, OBE, boomed through the theatre and left everyone including me exhausted. But the man who interested me most was Cameron Mackintosh. The *New York Times* described him at that time as the 'most successful, influential and powerful theatrical producer in the world'.

Adrian Reynold's plan was to take *Little Tramp* to the West End. If Mackintosh, a man who in his career produced *Les Misérables*, *Phantom of the Opera*, *Cats*, *Miss Saigon*, *Mary Poppins*, *Oliver!* and *Hamilton*, would come on board then the fortunes of the Haymarket would be secure. Or, as I put it to Adrian, if Mackintosh would not come on board then we might be lost.

We four, Mackintosh had a friend, met for lunch in a discreet London club where you have to be known at the door. It was a pleasant meal, but an uphill battle. Mackintosh was sold on the show, but it came down to money. The music and lyrics were by David Pomeranz; his demonstration tape alone was a knock out. But, and here I have to be careful, David was not seen to be his own man, we were told. Behind lay the Church of Scientology. This group of interconnected entities describes itself as a new religious movement. The church has been the subject of a number of controversies. It has been described by government inquiries, international parliamentary bodies, scholars and numerous superior court judgements as both a dangerous cult and a manipulative profit-making business. The church, we heard, wanted its cut and it wanted artistic control.

Mackintosh decided that he wanted out. After a vigorous discussion, he walked away.

Pomeranz did get his show on the stage again – at Waterford in Connecticut in 1995 and the following year in St Petersburg, Russia. Starved of the stage success he deserved with the full musical, Pomeranz turned *Little Tramp* into a one-man show, playing all forty plus characters himself, touring the United States and Australia. A celebrity studio album featured Richard Harris, Mel Brooks, Petula Clark, Tim Curry and, happily, Peter Duncan.

Pomeranz's wider music has sold over forty million copies worldwide with eighteen gold and twenty-two platinum records.

For my part, it was a missed opportunity and a great shame.

# LAURENCE SOPER, ET ALL

Monks, priests and abusers at St Benedict's School, Ealing

*Laurence Soper.* BBC.

I don't think that I ever met Andrew Soper, known as Father Laurence, which makes him an odd choice for one of the seventy famous people I have glimpsed and who were thought worthy of inclusion in *Wikipedia*.

But I well might have done.

Soper was one of a string of Benedictine monks, priests and teaching staff to face allegations of indecent assault against young boys over several decades at St Benedict's School in Ealing, West London. The charges officially stretched from the 1960s to the 2010s at the school which was attached to Ealing Abbey and also included offences against girls at St Gregory's Roman Catholic Primary School, a state school in Woodfield Road, Ealing, with links to the abbey and to the Order's Buckfast Abbey Preparatory School in Devon. Other offences occurred at Ampleforth College, Belmont Abbey, Douai Abbey, Downside Abbey and Worth Abbey.

In my personal experience, the abuse at St Benedict's extended from at least the late 1950s when I attended for a few years and was serially molested before being expelled for complaining. To make matters worse, my father sided with the official rejection of my claims, made when I was eleven years old, and beat me for my lies.

The Independent Inquiry into Child Sexual Abuse (IICSA) declared that a culture of cover-up and denial of sexual crime operated at the Abbey school. A group of ordained paedophiles behaved 'like mafia' over fifty years. The school was a 'grim and beastly place'. The IICSA received about twenty allegations against eight monks and staff, but suggested that the true scale was 'likely to be much higher'. Failings were also found amongst the police, the Crown Prosecution Service (CPS) and child protection teams.

Headmaster Laurence Soper may never have touched me while I was a pupil at St Benedict's from 1957 to 1959, but he makes a good example of the several monks who did. Soper, aged seventy-four, resigned as abbot in 2000 and moved to Rome as the victims started to come forward. He then fled to Kosovo for six years with £182,000 from the Vatican Bank in a bid to avoid prosecution for abusing boys while he faced a European Arrest Warrant. He was extradited to face nineteen charges of indecent and serious sexual assault against ten former pupils and was the fourth man to be convicted.

A request was sent to the Holy See for a witness statement on what steps were taken after Soper disappeared in 2011 which the Vatican declined to answer.

Prosecutor Gillian Etherton QC told how the victims were subjected to 'sadistic beatings' by Soper for 'fake reasons' and on many occasions 'with what can only have been a sexual motive'. These reasons included kicking a football in the wrong direction and using the wrong staircase.

The Old Bailey jury found Soper guilty of all charges.

Judge Anthony Bate said Soper's conduct, was the 'most appalling breach of trust' and that he had 'subverted the rules of the Benedictine Order and teachings of the Catholic Church'. His remaining years would now be 'overshadowed by the proven catalogue of his vile abuse'.

'You have been a clandestine sex offender since your early thirties. Your disgrace is complete.'

Soper was attacked while on remand at Wormwood Scrubs prison and, on sentencing, was segregated for his own protection.

Perhaps my abusers were among the others who were convicted:

- *In 2009, Father David Pearce, seventy-five, nicknamed the 'devil in a dog collar' was jailed when he admitted eleven charges of indecent assault dating back to 1972.*
- *Between 2003 and 2009, master of discipline John Maestri, seventy-eight, admitted five indecent assaults in the 1980s and was jailed.*
- *In 2011, Stephen Skelton was convicted of indecent assaults against two complainants in 1983.*
- *Peter Allott, a deputy head, was charged with downloading and distributing indecent images of children.*
- *Father Anthony Gee faced accusations of abuse and a civil action was brought against him.*

Staff who reported concerns against teacher behaviour compared it to 'ramming your head against a brick wall'. Peter Halsall, a teacher, complained 'but they didn't go anywhere and it definitely harmed my career'.

I don't think that the IICSA report ever uncovered the extent of the abuse, the number of staff involved or the full period the abuse covered. In my time, these activities were everywhere, well known and openly discussed among the boys. I suspect I was chosen around a dozen times. It is difficult to remember details after all these years. To be honest, while I didn't like it, it was not a devastating part of my life. Far worse happened later in prison. When you were called out for some minor misdemeanour, you knew what was coming. The senior staff used a thick tawse, a leather strap having one end cut into short thongs This was applied with a hefty swing to your bottom as you leant over the desk in the master's study. You were supposed to say, 'Thank you, Father', as you left the room fighting to hold your tears in front of the waiting queue of boys.

Normal punishment was up to six whacks. It was a short step to say 'yes' for a reduction to, say, three in return for dropping you pants and presenting your bare skin. The teacher then manoeuvred himself into position, by placing an arm around your back and either cupping your testicles or rubbing your penis. This approach also meant that the force of the blow was considerably lessened and there was quite a length of time between strikes. One teacher liked to stroke my anus.

It was as much for the unnecessary but incessant beating, as the molestation, that I complained. I found an odd way of raising my case: I came top of my year in mathematics, English and Latin and bottom in every other subject. When asked why, I said it was to do with staff playing with my penis. My abusers were so brazen and confident that a complaint was made to my father about my disrespect. With no support, indeed beatings at home (my father liked to hit me around the head), I was packed off to the local grammar school which had forsworn corporal punishment.

I soon forgot the episodes. I can honestly say that I am unaware of any scars, but that seems far from true of some of my fellow pupils.

One victim suffered from nightmares and flashbacks. Another said he was left faithless and suicidal. Later, he took to drinking to 'numb the pain of what was happening to him'. He had 'tried countless times' to take his life. He said he wanted to be a vet or a pilot before his life was ruined.

At least I did go on to become a pilot.

# ALEC JAMES STEWART

English international batsman, wicket-keeper and captain

# DAVID IVON GOWER

English international batsman and captain

*Alec Stewart, 2007.* Nick Richards.

*David Gower, 2011.* Liam Fitzpatrick, Flickr.

I was bowling my first over in, perhaps, twenty years. I thought off spin would be easiest to get into my stride. I bowled with my right arm and finger spin. The ball spun from left to right when it bounced on the dry pitch and into the newly-arrived right-handed batsman. I was quite pleased, the batsman, clearly inexperienced, had to step back sharply to block the ball.

'Straight onto the spot,' said the umpire. 'What are you going to do next?'

'Same again, I think. It'll give him false confidence.'

The umpire nodded and transferred one of six stones from one hand into a pocket.

It was a mirror second ball and the batsman was already stepping back as I bowled.

'Now, what?'

'I was thinking of a leg break, but if I bowl a good one after all this time, he'll probably just miss it altogether. I think another off break, but I'll try to pitch it six to eight inches further up the pitch with a little more bounce. If he plays the same shot automatically he may back into his wicket.'

And that's what happened. Batsman out for nought, hit wicket, bowled Heal. Big shout from me.

'What are you doing next week?' asked the umpire. 'We could do with another spin bowler at Surrey.'

I turned to face him, *The Gaffer*, Alec Stewart, who had not long made his Test debut for the England cricket team against the West Indies.

'I'm old enough to be your father,' I replied.

'Do you know who my father is?' he came back.

'I do. Micky who used to play a bit of cricket himself.' Micky Stewart, a Surrey stalwart, played several games as a right-handed batsman for England before his career was curtailed by ill health.

I bowled the fourth and fifth balls at the new batsman in a reprise of the start to the over.

'I'll try that leg break now, just to see if I can still do it.'

I couldn't and the ball went whizzing to the boundary for four. I was taken off after that as everyone was getting a bowl and it was an almost friendly game between a side from my consultancy company and an advertising agency with whom we worked called *Rhino*, 'thick skinned, horny and charges too much'.

One of the owners of Rhino was trying to broaden his product offering and had approached some of the leading English cricketers to see if he could represent and promote their interests. Negotiations seemed to be going well and two of them, Alec Stewart and David Gower, had agreed to come to the picturesque small ground at Lower Wield in Hampshire, on the other side of the country lane from the *The Yew Tree* pub and restaurant, where we had arranged to play our friendly. Stewart, not wanting to be far from the action, offered to umpire while Gower was in the clubhouse with the sandwiches and the ladies.

David Gower was nearing the end of his England career. Usually described as 'one of the most stylish left-handed batsmen of his era', he eventually played one hundred and seventeen Test matches and one hundred and fourteen One Day Internationals (ODIs) scoring 8,231 and 3,170 runs, respectively. He also captained England until two whitewashes against the West Indies lost him the job. In 2018, Gower was named in England's greatest Test XI.

As one might have expected, the two teams facing each other that day were full of overweight and slowing businessmen (and a few ladies to whom this did not apply) whose memories were greater than their feats. Except, I had included a ringer, my son, Arran, in our team. A sporting teenager, he almost gave the game away when he took a running, one-handed catch on a far boundary.

I arranged our batting order so that he and I were together at the crease with thirty runs needed. It was the only time that we played together. The bowling was poor and we quickly knocked off the runs until there were only four left to get. Arran was facing and I was keeping Gower company, now umpiring, at the other end. He had a bottle of cold white wine and a plate of sandwiches carefully protected by the wicket.

Arran straight-batted for four and the match was ours.

'That's my son,' I told Gower.

'Proud dad,' he replied. 'It was a nice catch, too.'

Then it was over the road to *The Yew Tree*.

# JOHN THOMSON STONEHOUSE

## British parliamentarian who faked his own death

Interviewing John Stonehouse was one of my first 'big' jobs on my weekly newspaper, the *Midland Chronicle*, based in West Bromwich. I got the assignment because a fellow reporter fell off his cycle the day before and was hit by a car. He was in hospital with a broken leg. I was twenty-one.

Stonehouse became a Labour and Co-operative Party member of parliament in a 1957 by-election in Wednesbury, a town just down the road from West Bromwich, for which we ran a slip edition. He quickly got into trouble and made both friends and enemies. He travelled to Rhodesia on a fact-finding tour during which he condemned the white minority government. He encouraged the African National Congress to stand up for their rights. He was promptly deported and banned from returning. In government as a junior minister of aviation, he fought against the British Overseas Airways Corporation (BOAC) decision to order Boeing 707 aircraft from the United States against his own recommendation that they should buy the British-made Vickers Super VC10.

*John Stonehouse, 1967.* City Archives of Toulouse.

We met in the bar of a posh local hotel. No one had authorised money for me to buy drinks, but I had no option. The interview was a mismatch, of course. I was the callow youth, he was the experienced politician of my father's generation. I read later that the political scientist Bernard Crick, a contemporary of Stonehouse at the London School of Economics, recalled his nickname was 'Lord John' and that his main conversation was always about how best to get a parliamentary seat.

I had done some homework and set out to establish some common ground. Stonehouse had just been made Minister, Post and Telecommunications, and I pointed out that my father was the head postmaster in West Bromwich. I knew that Stonehouse had been educated at Taunton's School, where an uncle of mine was sports master, but I got that one wrong to his amusement. His school was Taunton's (now Richard Taunton Sixth Form College) in Southampton, my uncle's was Taunton School in Somerset. Stonehouse had been a pilot in the RAF at the end of the war. I had briefly joined the RAF as a pilot and had flown commercially. My flight training included time on a Boeing 707 simulator at Feltham, the plane he had pressured BOAC not to buy.

It was a pleasant if uneventful late morning chat. He declined lunch much to my financial relief and gave me his business card in case I should want to check any details. I wrote the story and it disappeared into the sub-editors' room. I found it in the next issue of the paper with hardly any changes. No one mentioned it, neither at the newspaper nor from Stonehouse or his office.

Job done.

What makes Stonehouse particularly interesting came to light after my interview, in fact, after I had left the newspaper.

First, since 1962, Stonehouse was a Czechoslovak secret service agent. At that time, he was the only minister known to have worked clandestinely for the Eastern bloc. Stonehouse successfully, at least publicly, defended himself against allegations from a Czech defector. Maragaret Thatcher even sanctioned a cover up because there was insufficient evidence for a trial. However, in 2009, an official history of MI5 substantiated the story.[32]

Second, when Stonehouse lost his ministerial salary in 1970, he set up various companies and most of them were soon in trouble. The Department of Trade and Industry looked into his affairs and he began rehearsing a fake identity. This continued until, in 1974, he faked his death. He left a pile of clothing on a beach in Miami to make it appear that he had died while swimming. It was an international sensation. No corpse was found because Stonehouse was on his way to Australia with his mistress.

Third, in Australia, Stonehouse began moving large sums of money between bank accounts using further false identities. He was spotted and placed under surveillance. Local police thought Stonehouse might be Lord Lucan, the

---

32 Andrew, Christopher, *The Defence of the Realm* (2009).

missing peer who was suspected of murdering his children's nanny. Pictures of both fugitives were sent from London, but police asked Stonehouse to pull down his trousers to check whether he had Lucan's signature scar on his right thigh.

Stonehouse was literally caught with his pants down.

Stonehouse was sentenced to seven years for fraud after a sixty-eight day trial where he defended himself. He was declared bankrupt and served most of his time in Wormwood Scrubs. Later, he became a minor celebrity, writing three novels and making numerous radio and TV programmes including TVS's *Regrets* and the BBC Radio 4 interview programme *In the Psychiatrist's Chair* with Anthony Clare.

He really died in 1988 three weeks after collapsing on the TV set of an edition of *Central Weekend* in Birmingham during the filming of a programme about missing people.

# LHAMO THONDUP

## Jetsun Jamphel Ngawang Lobsang Yeshe Tenzin Gyatso, 14<sup>th</sup> Dalai Lama

Late in 1968, after the Paris riots, Diane, my wife, and I arrived in New Delhi having hitchhiked and bussed from the UK. The trip, taking in Yugoslavia, Turkey, Iran and Pakistan, is another story. India's capital was not immediately welcoming. It was hot, noisy and, it seemed, full of dust blown by strong winds. We also had very little money and nowhere to stay.

A chance meeting with a local student introduced us to an organisation known as SCI. From a poky, crowded office in a tiny back street, SCI placed young volunteers in manual labour schemes in the countryside. We were in luck as a month-long project was to start in a few days in Himachal Pradesh in the Himalayan foothills.

*Tenzin Gyatso, 14th Dalai Lama, 2012.* Flickr.

Shamipur, *windy village*, also sometimes Shamirpur, with a population of around one hundred and fifty, had no entry road passable, even by a four-wheel drive vehicle. Surplus crops could not be driven out to market and essential supplies could only be carried in by mule and backpack. It had ever been thus. The job was to widen two miles of mountain track using pickaxe and shovel to enable a connection to the nearest road. SCI would pay for the bus to a nearby stop and the villagers would provide accommodation in their homes and share their normal food.

To be accepted, we had to fill in, from memory, twelve different multi-page forms which took most of a day. I recall that even a cinema ticket stub from Pakistan was noted because it showed that we had supped with the devil. Three committees approved our application. As they separately debated our suitability, we sat at the back of the room where plaster dripped from the walls. We are accepted, but not without some suspicion and direct questioning about our motives. Almost all of the normal applications were from families which lived locally. We were unusual and, also, British.

While we waited to leave, we were offered free sleeping space and rope beds with a dozen others, all on different journeys, on the open roof of the apartment of a rich sponsor. We watched shooting stars and steady satellites through the night.

After many hours cramped with our packs on wooden benches on a very tired bus, we were dropped by an unremarkable roadside. Four villagers with two mules for baggage stirred themselves. They had waited for us for two days. We began what proved to be a long trek along the edges of rice fields and skirting poorly-tended tea plantations as we climbed the Kangra valley. The sun was blistering and there was no water. Rice rats scurried among the baked paddies. Unseen monkeys complained from beyond the treeline. After the first hour, it was all uphill on a stone single-file track where green and brown snakes slithered out of our path.

Shamipur was a poor village without power which proudly boasted an almost new single-room school for all ages. Water came from a hand pump in the grassy central courtyard. Washing meant filling a hefty clay pitcher and emptying it over one's head. All the while we were watched closely by several village ladies who, we were told, had never before seen white skin. Diane and I had our own small tent which was seen, by some, as elitist. We were scheduled to stay with all the others in an empty hut with an earth floor where blankets were provided. Food, except for the occasional special day with a wealthy family, was monotonous and meatless: chapatis and potato for breakfast and chapatis, potatoes and, perhaps, rice with dahl for dinner. There was cholera in one of the houses.

We worked hard digging away at the hillside and moving boulders, pebbles, tree roots and earth with hands which quickly blistered. On most days, some of the villagers came to watch. Our 'chief engineers' were two enthusiastic West Germans waiting to go to university who planned each phase of the widening like experienced construction managers. Female workers were restricted by convention to working in pairs shifting small rocks and pushing wheelbarrows. A few volunteers slipped away during the first week.

We learned that the Germans had applied to make a special visit to the small town of Dharamsala. Diane and I elbowed our way into their outing. Permission came through by a hand-written message deliver by a runner. We took a full day's break from our labours and left at five on a cold mountain morning with hanging grey clouds brushing the top of gully walls.

At Dharamsala, it was an unexceptional scene, a planned meeting in a well-kept garden, except that our host did not see us arrive. As our small party entered, the man's back was turned to us as he faced his gardener. Clearly, something had upset him badly with the work done or not done amongst the rhododendrons. He let fly, not in English or Urdu, with a torrent of lengthy and detailed abuse. The gardener wilted visibly. His head sank into his shoulders and tears fell.

Some sixth sense suggested to our host that he was not alone. He turned. His face shifted instantly from anger to the utmost serenity. His palms joined in a formal greeting of *Namaskar* to show respect. The tips of his fingers were thus joined to the pressure points of his eyes, ears and mind so that we, his audience, would know that we would be remembered for a long time.

That was how I met the man born as Llamo Thondup, now the highest spiritual leader and head of Tibetan Buddhism, the 14th Dalai Lama, Jetsun Jamphel Ngawang Lobsang Yeshe Tenzin Gyatso.

Recovered from his outburst, the Dalai Lama received five thin, white linen prayer scarfs from an attendant, blessed them as a bunch, and they were taken back and passed one to each of our party. After a perfunctory communal blessing, His Holiness turned on his heels and slipped through an adjacent curtained doorway. The attendant now performed the role of beshawled interpreter and answered a few stuttering and unprepared questions from the two West Germans and then he, too, pivoted and was gone.

We stood with our individual scarves laying over our wrists, looking at the shrivelled gardener, and pondered the planning and effort that had gone into our six-hour journey by foot, mule and cramped bus full of chickens and goats. We stumbled out into the afternoon sun, spinning Buddhist prayer wheels which lined the tracks, and found a small front room which sold noodle soup, without chapatis or potatoes, for a few pence. I also bought some chocolate.

Tenzin Gyatso, his spiritual name, was born in 1935 to a farming family in the village of Taktser in Tibet, near the Chinese frontier. Following reported sightings and visions, three search teams were sent out to find the new reincarnation. Two years later, Gyatso was selected as the *tulku*, the successor of the 13th Dalai Lama and, in 1939, formally recognised as such. The Chinese authorities repeatedly sought to interfere and profit from the appointment. The following year, Chinese forces annexed Tibet.

Aged eleven, Gyatso met the Austrian mountaineer Heinrich Farrer who taught him about the word outside Lhasa. When he was nineteen, Gyatso toured China for almost a year meeting many of the revolutionary leaders including Mao Zedong. During the 1959 Tibetan uprising against Chinese rule, the Dalai Lama escaped to India with the help of the CIA (US Central Intelligence Agency) and eventually settled in Dharamsala, *Little Lhasa*, from where he travels the world meeting and speaking on a wide range of humanitarian subjects. He was awarded the Nobel Peace Prize in 1989 and, since then, many other world-wide honours.

Gyatso's tenure has often courted criticism, especially from the Chinese. His views on sexuality have shifted from his trenchant 'right organ in the right object at the right time'. He has described himself as a Marxist. He claims 'people think of animals as if they were vegetables, and that is not right'.

Many years later, I searched the attic for my prayer scarf. I knew it had made it back with me to the UK, but it was nowhere to be found.

# PAUL TORTELIER

## French cellist and composer

It was, perhaps, 1987 so Paul Tortelier would have been about seventy-three-years-old, three years from his death. Tortelier was a world-renowned cellist who had just given a successful performance of the Elgar Cello Concerto at a concert in Aberdeen. A group of some forty people were enjoying a post concert dinner held by the event's corporate sponsor for their local customers. Tortelier sat next to my wife and, under the cover of the tablecloth, he groped her leg.

Tortelier was French, also a composer, and came to fame after an outstanding studentship from the age of twelve at the Conservatoire de Paris. He played in local orchestras and in the USA before the war.

*Paul Tortelier.*

After the war ended, he became a well-known soloist, taught at music schools in France, Germany and China and gave televised masterclasses in England.

He began his solo career in Berlin and Amsterdam, where a performance of Richard Strauss's Don Quixote caught the ear of Sir Thomas Beecham, the conductor. Tortelier was invited for a reprise at London's Wigmore Hall.

Tortelier played with many of the household names in the classical music world. In 1950, Pablo Casals asked him play as principal cellist in the Prades Festival Orchestra, then an isolated Catalan village. Casals said, 'When you play you make [the cello] talk.' At a concert to mark his own seventy-fifth birthday, Tortelier was joined by his friend Mstislav Rostropovich.

Tortelier reported that he found the English baffling because of their undemonstrative feelings, but he was 'fond of them'.

'I cannot speak of the English without emotion,' he said. 'I owe them everything in terms of my career.' He was less at home with Americans who he found friendly but lacking in real love.

Tortelier had a short-lived marriage to Madelaine Gaston which ended in divorce in 1944. Two years later, he married a cello pupil, Maud Monique Martin, with whom he had three children, Yan Pascal, a violinist and later conductor, Maria de la Pau, a pianist, and Pomona, a cellist. Although he was not Jewish but an agnostic Roman Catholic, Tortelier was inspired by the ideals of the founders of the newly-formed state of Israel and for a while from 1955 lived with his wife and children in the kibbutz Ma'abarot near Haifa.

So, there was no doubt that Tortelier, the man who had molested my wife in a sneaky way believing he would get away with it, was a man of great musical standing. He was also my guest; I was paying the bills. My wife reported the incident to me, perhaps more surprised than anything. The interference was over and would not be repeated. She was safe in a room full of people. There can scarcely be a woman who has not had a series of similar unwanted advances in her life, many with much more serious consequences, and had needed to develop a mechanism for coping. In fact, this was her second such incident at a classical concert.

I saw Tortelier taking his leave of some casual admirers. I went over to him. Age, status, whatever, I did not think his sly self gratification should go unremarked.

I stood square before him and looked in the old man's rheumy eyes.

'You touched my wife's leg when you thought no one would see you and nothing would be said.'

He held my gaze and seemingly dared me to make a fuss.

'I am Paul Tortelier,' he said. 'Who are you?'

He turned and moved on to talk to the Lord Provost of Aberdeen.

'Not a coward,' was the best I could come up with in my personal moment. I'm not sure if he heard me, but I think he did.

Tortelier died of a heart attack in 1990, aged seventy-six, near Paris. At a commemorative concert, Yehudi Menuhin, Sir Charles Grove and Yan-Pascal Tortelier, his son, conducted. The cellists included Maud Martin Tortelier, his second wife, János Starker and two of Tortelier's former students, Arto Noras and Raphael Sommer.

# SIAOSI TÁUFA'ÁHAU TUPOULAHI
## TÁufa'Áhau Tupou IV, King of Tonga

The King of Tonga, Tāufa'āhau Tupou IV, apologised to me.

'Sorry for bothering you,' he said and waved his hand. Regally, Queen Elizabeth style.

I wasn't bothered at all, more impressed, but I certainly didn't want to appear churlish. I waved back, but in a more plebeian way. He was an affable sort of guy.

'No problem, sir.' I wish I could have found a more original reply but, when you're under social pressure, you live with what you have.

*Tāufa'āhau Tupou IV.*

My wife and I were on our way from Los Angeles to Fiji. We sat alone upstairs in a funny sort of Club bubble compartment (we had more money and better health in those days). My son, Arran, and his (first) wife waited at a sticky and fly-swept Nadi airport on the main island of Viti Levu for us to join them on a one-week holiday. This had all been arranged casually many months ago when we decided to give them a round-the-world ticket (economy) as their honeymoon present. A boat with chugging outboard and sleepy crew waited patiently to take us to a small island which an American couple had leased and then built an embryonic holiday resort of wooden bungalows on stilts. It rained with a vengeance all through almost every daylight hour, only relenting in the early evening to release a well-trained mosquito militia. I remember fondly the leatherback turtles climbing the beach, my son's first dive with sharks and the house speciality, a large cinnamon roll. On the way back to the mainland, the sun finally broke cover and Arran and I played a round at the Fiji Golf Club, which I won by an authoritative two strokes.

I should mention that the trip was early in 1997, but had been booked over a year before. Friends were amazed and respectful as I had arranged the whole thing on the internet, then a creepy crawly sloth of a thing. Talk about an 'early adapter'.

News crackled over the PA system on the plane. There would be a slight diversion. Instead of flying direct to Fiji, we would make a stop at Tonga, just an extra 500 miles. Why? Well, if you're the King of Tonga, it's a bit like ordering a taxi.

So that's why my pal, good old Tāufaʻāhau Tupou, apologised to me. He'd taken over an hour out of my life and then disturbed our solitary occupation of club class.

The king sat on the left as we were already on the right. Here's where the impressiveness came in. He was a big man. I mean 'big'. *Wikipedia* calls him the tallest and heaviest Tongan monarch. I agree with their research. He was six feet five inches, which is OK, just three inches taller than me. But, he weighed in at over four hundred and sixty pounds (two hundred and ten kilograms). He had a few flunkies and they were needed as he forced his way up the stairs. He squashed into two seats without an intervening arm rest. Could this diversion have been a regular affair?

In a country which views great physical size as beautiful, Tāufaʻāhau Tupou took his kingly responsibilities extremely seriously, taking a bottle of Tabasco sauce with him wherever he went. When the much travelled monarch visited Germany, the government used to commission special chairs that could support his weight. The king used to take them home, considering them state presents.

His weight was all the more remarkable because, as a youthly prince, he was one of Tonga's top athletes. A proficient pole vaulter who regularly climbed more than ten feet, he also played tennis, cricket, rugby, surfed, dived and rowed competitively.

And, then, the queen, a distant relative whom he married in 1947, was levered up the stairs. Well!

Tāufaʻāhau Tupou IV was the absolute ruler of more than one hundred and seventy Polynesian islands which were brought together when their many different tribal groups united in 1845. Though still the object of great reverence, the Tongan royal family faced criticism for enriching itself while most of its subjects remained in poverty. They also faced calls for greater democracy. Towards the end of the king's reign, authoritarianism increased, including the banning of independent overseas Press.

Tupou IV suffered from heart and age-related problems. He died in 2006 in hospital in Auckland, New Zealand, after reigning for forty-one years. There was a month-long period of national mourning. He was succeeded by his eldest son, George Tupou V.

When we landed at Fiji, the king and entourage, of course, left the plane first. There was a frantic moment as he was lowered down the stairwell. I thought for one heavy moment that he was stuck and that our rainy holiday was in jeopardy.

# HARRY WAXMAN

## English cinematographer

Harry Waxman was one of those famous people that few have heard of, but most people saw his work. Born in 1912, he started a career in film at British International Pictures as a camera assistant working at studios like Ealing, Welwyn and Worton Hall, also known as Isleworth. During the war, he served with the RAF Film Unit. In 1945, he photographed his first feature, *Journey Together*, under director John Boulting.[33] His work led to a contract with Two Cities Films in 1946. The next year, at Denham, he worked closely with the Boulting Brothers on two applauded productions:

*Harry Waxman.*

- *Associate cameraman: Fame is the Spur, based on the book by Howard Spring and starring Michael Redgrave, about a young man, supposedly based on Ramsay MacDonald, from a northern mill town committed to help the poverty-stricken workers in his area. He rises as a Labour MP, but is seduced by the trappings of power and finds himself the type of politician he originally despised.*

---

33 Petrie, Duncan, *The British Cinematographer* (BFI, 1996).

- *Cinematographer: Brighton Rock*, starring Richard Attenborough as Pinky, a vicious gangster, based on a Graham Greene thriller, and set in Brighton.

'While minor projects tended to come his way, Waxman did photograph some arresting films' notably *The Sleeping Tiger* (1954, Dirk Bogarde), the first British film of McCarthy blacklisted director and Communist party member Joseph Losey; and *Sapphire* (1959, Nigel Patrick, directed by Basil Dearden) for which Waxman won an award from the British Society of Cinematographers.

During the 1960s and 70s, Waxman worked on several atmospheric horror films like *The Nanny* (1965), *The Anniversary* (1967), both with Bette Davis, and on the cult classic *The Wicker Man* (1973) in which policeman Edward Woodward investigated a disappearance on a Hebridean island.

Waxman's considerable experience also landed second unit work on major productions such as *Khartoum* (1966, Charlton Heston and Laurence Olivier) and *A Bridge Too Far* (1977, directed by Richard Attenborough). Altogether, I count over sixty film credits as director of photography, including *Robbery Under Arms* (1957), *Swiss Family Robinson* (1960), *The Day the Earth Caught Fire* (1961), *Crooks in Cloisters* (1964), *She* (1965), *There's a Girl in My Soup* (1970) and *The Pink Panther Strikes Again* (1976).

Waxman was badly hit by the slump in the film industry in the 1970s and reduced to mediocre assignments such as TV spin-offs and sex comedies.

Which is when I met him, briefly and under a promise of secrecy.

At the time, I was working for a large American company and was closely involved in organising an MBO (management buyout) of their marketing communications department of which I was the manager. The multi-million pound deal involved many quiet meetings with potential investors and one such took place at an up-market Chinese restaurant in Richmond, Surrey, thought to be sufficiently off the beaten track from the usual haunts of London marketing companies. My guest was the deputy chairman of a leading European advertising agency.

Just as the main dishes were served, my partner asked, 'Do you realise you are being watched by that couple on the other side of the room?'

I looked up and realised it was my Auntie Louie, my mother's youngest sister, whom I had not seen for many years.

A word on my Auntie Louie, always one of our black sheep, whose amorous adventures were talked about by the extended family in hushed tones. Naturally flirtatious, good looking and well endowed, several prominent men friends were rumoured. I knew her two children better than I knew her. Scarcely clad photographs of her as an aspiring model used to be passed quietly to and fro, or hidden, as the interest took. Louie was looking at me in horror.

'She's coming over. Do you want me to disappear for a few minutes?'

Louie arrived, ready to do a deal.

'Hello, nephew,' she said. 'It looks like we've both been caught.'

Louise didn't leave me space to introduce or explain my very attractive guest. I quickly knew it would make no difference.

'Come and meet Harry,' she invited in a way that clearly meant me alone.

Harry Waxman was shifting nervously on his seat as he was introduced. I didn't know him from Adam. He looked, indeed was, older than my father, a few newish double chins and curly hair starting to recede.

'I wouldn't want this to get out,' said Louie,' not with everything that's going on. I guess you might feel the same.'

'Louie, don't worry,' I replied. 'My lips are sealed. We never met and my dinner is getting cold. Nice to meet you, Harry.' I turned and left.

Some time later, Louie married Harry after her divorce came through. Harry died soon after and she married again. Louie herself died many years ago now otherwise I would not be telling this story. She never did get into the movies. And, yes, my buyout did happen later that year, but without the participation of the lady I dined with that evening.

# PRINCE CHARLES PHILIP ARTHUR GEORGE WINDSOR
King Charles III

# NIGEL CORBALLY-STOURTON
Irish hunting and fishing soldier and royal go-between

*Prince Charles, 1982, and his mother.*

*Nigel Corbally-Stourton, late Grenadier Guards.*

I apologise for ending this book as I started with a story based on IBM. However, I did work for the company for about twenty years. After my first flush, it seemed I was always looking to leave, but got trapped by regular enticements: money, new positions, foreign homes, rank, flattery and travel. Nowadays, I find it all a bit embarrassing. I suspect I am largely alone amongst my peers in that, on balance, I regret my employment.

This is the final chapter of my effort to shrug off my time in hospital because the famous chap I met had the surname 'Windsor', previously 'Mountbatten' from his German forebears, and it is alphabetically last on the list.

In 1980, I worked in Buchan House in St Andrew Square, Edinburgh, two eighteenth century homes carefully and expensively renovated as offices in the middle of the city's financial district. The time came for an official opening when all of Scotland's great and good could be assembled and impressed and I was appointed to manage the nuts and bolts of the affair. Approaches were made to the royal household for a suitable 'opener'. Prince Charles, after much negotiation, agreed to the commission. There was great excitement.

I say 'much negotiation' because at that time, IBM had in its head office, perhaps its most unusual employee called Nigel Corbally-Stourton. He is qualified on his own to claim one of my chapters.

I met him first in London on the afternoon I interviewed to join the company. As I sat on a deep sofa in an impressive departmental reception, a character, I can only say like Alice's 'Mad Hatter', rushed to and fro, flapping his arms wildly and shouting to nobody and everybody, 'I'm late. I'm late. I must have a taxi now. Betty doesn't like it when people are late for tea.'

At interview, I checked. 'Betty' was, of course, Queen Elizabeth.

Nigel came from the deepest old Irish stock (Lords Killeen, Mowbray, Segrave and Stourton) with courageous ancestors in the Grenadier Guards in all recent wars, educated at Ampleforth and Sandhurst, and disgustingly well connected, playing polo at Smith's Lawn, Windsor, with the Duke of Edinburgh, The Prince of Wales and Prince William of Gloucester, and on and on went the list. Over twenty-five years, he made a career at IBM of his royal connections and of his interest in matters of social concern: the environment, arts, the disabled and generally saving the planet.

There were problems and I speak from, mostly, fondness. Nigel was not the best finisher. In fact, he could barely finish a sentence through excitement or boredom. He often upset people with his dramatic changes of direction. At core was, may be, the fact that, at Sandhurst, at one time he lay 190 out of 192 cadets. Of course, he still earned a short-service commission with the Regiment, based initially at Windsor.

My favourite Nigel story concerned a visit by Queen Elizabeth to IBM's new headquarters on reclaimed land at Cosham near Portsmouth. Nigel was on the organising committee, but the senior managers became so frustrated with his new demands from, supposedly, the palace that he was banned. He was told in the bluntest fashion that no one believed any more that he had serious royal contacts and his advice was not needed. I saw him leave the room, shoulders slumped, aghast.

Come the day, Nigel had snuck in and was hiding behind a pillar as the Queen worked her way along the line of dignitaries. Nigel popped his face out, the Queen saw him and waved.

'Hello, Nigel,' she called.

So, for the Edinburgh opening, Nigel and I had some tense moments. For example, there was to be a prestigious lunch when Charles's food and wine preferences would dictate the menu. What we planned to eat was changed five times. Central to the argument was the correct balance between dill and tarragon in the classic *sauce verte* destined to accompany wild Scottish salmon. The hotel told me their head chef alternated between tears and walking out. Nigel had no conception of the downstream disruption, even anger, that he caused with his dithering. Halfway through the planning, I began to ignore his 'royal' requirements while listening politely to his almost daily phone calls.

Come the day, the building tour went smoothly. Pressure off, I was waiting with guests in an hotel anteroom for the Prince to arrive by specially-burnished lift. Nigel bustled up.

'I've asked Prince Charles and he is anxious to meet you as the organiser,' he said. 'It is a great honour. Please wait here.'

And off he went.

I have a great antipathy to the landowning classes. Nigel himself was a Plantagenet and they were predominant in, for instance, my current county, Hampshire, with just one hundred and sixty-four people owning over sixty per cent of the land. The crown with its duchies of Cornwall and Lancaster was the biggest landowner in the country.[34] The whole edifice was little changed from the Norman Conquest.[35]

The concept of a ruling royal family, leaders descending by birthright, is anathema. In practice, what more dysfunctional family could there be than the Windsors? And, yet, the Queen had done a remarkable job, providing much needed stability and common sense. The alternative could be shocking.

---

34 Heal, Chris, *Ropley's Legacy*, Chapter 12, pp. 213-229 (C&S 2021).
35 Heal, Chris, *The Winchester Tales* (C&S 2022).

It is not idle to speculate who might have risen to the top of the dung heap if elections were held for a president. The options would inevitably have been failed politicians who brought partiality and incompetence to every move. Tony Blair, anyone? Name your poison.

I didn't want to meet Charles, curtsy before him and utter inanities, pretending he was my chosen sovereign.

Nigel had dropped me in it. I was ushered forward, lackies and IBM management grinning. The prince, a year younger than me but born in Buckingham Palace, and I shook hands limply.

'Congratulations on a very smooth event,' he said. 'How long did you take to plan it all?'

I told him three months.

'Good heavens, I hope not.' He laughed. I didn't. We chatted for perhaps a minute about some aspect of his tour of our building and then it was someone else's turn. It was all smooth and professional and my moment was past.

Later, many people asked what Charles was like.

'Sad,' I said. 'He looked at heart like he wished he was anywhere else. And he seemed lonely. I felt when I talked to him that what he could really do with was being taken down the pub for a chat with ordinary people.'

Nigel strode up, full of himself. 'You'll remember that for the rest of your life,' he boasted. I will but not for the reasons he thought.

Charles is now king and has, perhaps, a limited time to live as he has cancer. In his authorised biography by Jonathan Dimbleby, Charles's parents were described as 'physically and emotionally distant'.[36] The Duke of Edinburgh was blamed for his disregard of Charles's sensitive nature, including forcing him to attend Gordonstoun school where he was bullied. The tribulations of his marriage to Diana Spencer are notorious. I met one of her close admirers, the rugby player and England captain Will Carling in Jersey at a conference some years later, but that's another story, not told here.

Nigel married a second wife, Lavinia, in 1995. She was the widow of Edmund Roche, 5th Baron Fermoy, who was the maternal uncle of Princess Diana. Fermoy suffered from long-term depression and shot himself at his home in Hungerford, aged forty-five.

---

36 Dimbleby, Jonathan, *The Prince of Wales* (William Morrow, 1994).

In an obituary for Nigel, Lavinia's son wrote: 'Horses played a large part in Nigel's and Lavinia's lives well into their late seventies. They rode in Botswana, India, South Africa, South America and the USA, and canoed the Zambezi. Nigel shot well and stalked on the west coast for forty years. He caught salmon or sea trout in twenty-four rivers, but failed to make his target of thirty … Together they made lovely gardens at their homes at Axford House near Malmesbury and The Old Vicarage, Sherston, both in Wiltshire, the Cotswolds, and in Spain.'[37]

Nigel died, aged eighty-seven, in 2024. I am sure this is where he would like to have been: in a story alongside the monarch.

St Andrew Square was transformed from the home of Edinburgh's traditional banking and insurance companies to became a centre of retail and leisure entertainment. IBM moved out of Buchan House and the building stood empty for many years, a costly white elephant.[38] In 2017, plans were announced to turn the premises into a seventy-two room hotel with restaurants and bars. You can visit it now as *Malmaison Edinburgh City* – 'discover luxury and comfort'. Peak daily rates are £445.

---

37 Fermoy, The Lord, 'Obituary', *The Guards Magazine,* Spring 2025.
38 'The transformation of St Andrew Square', *The Scotsman,* 27/9/2017.

Chris Heal's books are available through major internet booksellers. Find details at www.candspublishing.org.uk.

### *Sound of Hunger* (2018)

*An acclaimed social biography of two brothers, Erich and Georg Gerth, WW1 u-boat captains, set against Germany's political and militaristic development from Bismarck to Hitler. A fast-paced, true detective story that tracks across archives, places and events in Europe and Africa. A selected book in several German universities for its surprising English perspective.*

### *Disappearing* (2019)

*A nomad with a violent past, infuriated by petty bureaucracy and the surveillance society, determines to live happily ever after, throwing off identity and leaving no trace. Things go awry: fighting for Biafran secessionists, gun running in Morocco, murder in Brussels, terrorists in Nairobi and a deathly Saharan escape. Semi-autobiographical.*

### *Reappearing* (2020)

*The semi-autobiographical sequel to* Disappearing. *If an elderly couple save you from a bad death in the Sahara, there's an honest debt to be paid. But this couple have conflicting plans. The only escape is down the River Niger where some unpleasant people await. The hunt is on for an elusive father who fought for the French across the globe in the dog days of empire.*

### *The Four Marks Murders* (2020) (*first part of the Ridge Trilogy*)

*In this true-life thriller, Chris Heal investigates deliberate and untimely deaths in what was thought to be one of the quiet backwaters of Hampshire. The twenty murders begin in Roman times with over half since 1900 and three within the last few years. They beg the question, 'Is Four Marks the murder capital of Southern England?'*

### *Ropley's Legacy* (2021) (*second part of the Ridge Trilogy*)

The Ridge Enclosures, 1709 to 1850: Chawton, Farringdon, Medstead, Newton Valence and Ropley and the birth of Four Marks.

*The first private parliamentary enclosure in England was in 1709 in Ropley. Driven by the less than saintly bishop of Winchester, it was a highly contested land grab seeking to make money by taking control of the common fields. Over 150 years, the government sanctioned theft spread to all the neighbouring ridge villages. A detailed history.*

### *The Winchester Tales* (2022) *(concluding part of the Ridge Trilogy)*

An Anglo-Norman love story set during the invasion of England after 1066.

*Gilbert of Bayeux, orphan, linguist and administrator, is brought to Winchester by Bishop Odo in 1067 to mastermind the appropriation of the land of the Saxon thegns fallen at Hastings. For the next forty years, he treads a precarious path through the Norman occupation. His great love, Ailgifu, is an outspoken mead seller from Medstead. His servant, Lēofric, provides challenging and dangerous company.*

### **Bad Moon Rising** (2023)

Three disturbing short stories about despair.

*Disgraced soldier Billy Budd returns to Alton in Hampshire having lost all belief in authority. His great wish is to destroy those who make the rules. Mary May is a recently widowed pensioner without family or close friends. Much of the overworked welfare community has retreated behind websites. The Russians deploy nuclear weapons in Ukraine to disastrous effect. Two survivors aboard the international space station are flung into the great void.*

### **The War of the Raven** (2023)

The career of Kapitänleutnant Georg Gerth 1888-1970.

*Georg Gerth volunteered for u-boat command to counter England's attempt to starve Germany into submission. His patrols took him into the North Sea, the English Channel and the French Atlantic. Stranded south of Calais, his boat proved a trove of intelligence. He was imprisoned, tried to escape, but was incarcerated as a pawn until the Versailles Treaty. His story is backed by extensive research and private interviews with his descendants.*

### **Saints & Sinners** (2023)

The career of Kapitänleutnant Erich Gerth 1886-1943.

*Between the world wars, three powerful men befriended the young u-boat captain, Erich Gerth, all vehemently anti-communist and on the far right of German politics: master spy Wilhelm Canaris, Admiral Adolf von Trotha and 'Consul' Salomon Marx, Jewish powerbroker. Gerth's career and life was doomed by his marriage to a young widow, Gräfin Eva von Ahlefeldt. The story is backed by extensive research and private interviews with his family.*

### **La dernière patrouille de l'UC 61** (2023) with Henri Lesoin

A French view of the last patrol of Georg Gerth's u-boat, UC 61.

*The story, based largely on Chris Heal's books,* Sound of Hunger *and* The War of the Raven, *has been translated into French and updated by Lt. Col. Henri Lesoin and his naval and community colleagues in Wissant, the site of the boat's stranding. Lesoin has introduced many additional photographs and insights.*

www.ingramcontent.com/pod-product-compliance
Lightning Source LLC
Chambersburg PA
CBHW061230070526
44584CB00030B/4062